Miniature
Embroidery
for the Georgian
Dolls' House

Miniature Embroidery
for the Georgian Dolls' House

Pamela Warner

Guild of Master Craftsman Publications Ltd

First published in 1999 by
Guild of Master Craftsman Publications Ltd,
166 High Street, Lewes,
East Sussex, BN7 1XU

ISBN 1 86108 136 7

A catalogue record of this book is available from the British Library

Photography and cover photograph by Zul Mukhida except Figs 1.1, 1.2, 1.3, 1.4, 1.5,
13.2, 13.5, 13.7, 13.8, 13.9 and 15.2, by Pamela Warner

Charts produced by Peter Rhodes

Black-and-white line drawings by John Yates, from sketches by Pamela Warner,
except drawings in the Stitch Glossary, by Pamela Warner

Colour drawings and patterns © Pamela Warner

Designed by Teresa Dearlove

Typeface: Perpetua

Colour origination by Viscan Graphics (Singapore)
Printed and bound by Kyodo Printing (Singapore) under the supervision of MRM
Graphics, Winslow, Buckinghamshire, UK

With sincere thanks to my students, past and present, for their friendship and support.

Acknowledgements

The frames for the samplers, Designs 1 to 7 (Chapter 8) are by Adam Syred, aged 10, Wood Supplies. The Chinoiserie pole and fire screens are mounted in kits by John Brace, Anglesey Dolls' Houses. All other furniture and frames are by the author.

Note on Measurements

Throughout, measurements are given in both metric and imperial systems. Please use only one system for each project as the two are equivalents only and are not exact.

T HE GEORGIAN era is a very popular choice for miniaturists and collectors. Many kits and ready-made dolls' houses are available in variations of this style, and they can be decorated to reflect any of the different styles that evolved during the long period included in the term 'Georgian'.

A visit to a restored house or museum will show that the elegance of the eighteenth century lends itself to the use of embroidered items. I have based many of the projects included here on authentic pieces, and although the designs have been simplified to allow a reduction in scale, they still retain the spirit of the originals.

My own collection of houses includes two in the Georgian style, and they gave me particular pleasure to make and decorate. I enjoyed using the light pastel shades and delicate mouldings. The first, a five-storey town house, is decorated mainly to the year 1740. As I wanted to include a bathroom, however, I had to allow it to be occupied by a Victorian family. The second, as yet unfinished, is a grander country house, c.1760, with a sweeping staircase and large, elegant rooms.

Many of you will not necessarily want to date your houses so precisely, which leaves you the freedom to use any of the projects at will. For those of you who wish to be more authentic, I have dated the projects where possible. Many, however, could be used throughout the period, as a house in the country would be slower to change than one in the centre of a major city. It is possible, of course, to have an earlier artefact in a house which may have been 'handed down', or you can have an early house with later occupants and contents, as I have with my town house.

The first volume in this series, *Miniature Embroidery for the Victorian Dolls' House*, contains projects for the period 1837–1910. This volume covers the period 1702–1830 and will be followed by one with Tudor and Stuart projects, and later by a volume covering the twentieth century.

Making miniature embroidery is very satisfying. Whether you are a beginner or an experienced stitcher, and whether you have a dolls' house, room box or simple display area, I hope you enjoy trying out the projects in this book as much as I enjoyed designing and making them for you.

Introduction

1 Influences on design and style

The projects included in this book range through the eighteenth and into the early nineteenth century. The Georgian period was sandwiched between the reigns of Queen Anne (1702–14) and William IV (1830–7), who was followed by Victoria (1837–1901). The overall Georgian style can be divided as shown in the following table.

Date	Monarch	Design style
1702–14	Anne	Queen Anne
1714–27	George I	Early Georgian
1727–60	George II	Georgian
1760–1812	George III	Late Georgian
1812–20		Regency
1820–30	George IV	Late Regency

The eighteenth century was a time of progress in science, learning and early mechanization. An increase in commerce created a new, wealthy middle class of merchants and traders. With this increase in prosperity, many prestigious country houses and estates were built, as well as elegant houses in the towns, spas and cities ranging from the large and affluent to smaller, more comfortable dwellings. Houses were arranged on two, three or more levels. Single-fronted houses had two rooms, one behind the other, with the entrance hall and stairs off to one side on each level. Double-fronted houses had two rooms either side of the central entrance hall and stairs to each level.

Early eighteenth-century house design continued to reflect the high Baroque of the previous century, with heavily gilded, ornate carving and statuary used both inside and outside. This was followed by the Rococo style, influenced by the French court, with its pastel colours, lighter gilding, delicate carving and the extensive use of mirrors.

The Palladian style of architecture followed in the period c.1714–60. This new style was Italian in influence, with distinctive porticoes and columns. The 'Queen Anne' style was not eclipsed by this Italianate style and continued well after her reign, typified by a sense of balance, well-placed windows, broad, shallow staircases with elegant balustrades, and plain panelling in the ground-floor reception rooms.

The elegant Adam and Neo-classical styles of architecture and interior decoration and furnishings, depicting classical urns with wreaths and swags of flowers, became popular around 1760 and continued into the 1790s. In contrast, after the middle of the century the 'Gothick' style was also in vogue, with pointed arches, mock-medieval features and castellated exterior decoration.

Fig 1.1 Below left **A fragment of silk embroidery on linen, mid-eighteenth century. The naturalistic flowers and light, open style is typical of the Georgian period.**

Fig 1.2 Below **Detail of Fig 1.1.**

Towards the end of the eighteenth century, during the 1780s and '90s, there was a revival inspired by Ancient Greek style, made popular by the architect James Wyatt. This was followed by the Regency style, known in America as the 'Federal style'.

Further information on the architecture and interior design of these styles can be found in the many books that are available on restoration, furniture, architecture, interior design and museum collections. It is also useful to look at contemporary paintings. The local library is a good starting point for reference books.

Many of the larger furnishing items found in fashionable houses would have been made in professional workshops. Embroidery for the European market was also produced in great quantities in India and the Far East, using European designs which were often interpreted with an Indian or Chinese flavour.

Embroidery was also a very popular and socially acceptable occupation for ladies at all levels of Georgian society and played an important part in the display of status and wealth. Ladies also learned to paint and draw, which in turn gave them a knowledge of nature and botany. This influenced the designs they used for many of the embroidered items. Magazines were readily available to keep them informed of the latest ideas and fashions.

Fig 1.3 **Eighteenth-century embroidery in fine silk thread.**

Fig 1.4 **Part of a bed valance on linen twill with chain stitch in fine wool, eighteenth century. Probably worked in India for the European market.**

Fig 1.5 **Detail of Fig 1.4.**

During the eighteenth century a wide range of embroidery techniques were used. Canvaswork, being durable, was widely used on practical items such as cushions, carpets and screens, as well as for decorative wall hangings and pictures. Silk embroidery using naturalistic colours was also used for pictures, bedcovers and costumes. Knotting, quite a craze during the eighteenth century, was ideal for curtains and hangings. Quilting also attained great status at this time, and was used for bedcovers and clothes along with patchwork.

Greater detail on these techniques is given in the introductions to the individual chapters and projects.

THE PROJECTS are all presented in 1/12 scale as this is the most popular in use today. Instructions for working projects to 1/24 scale are basically the same, but guidance on alternative fabrics and the number of threads to use is given in Chapter 12. Patterns can be reduced on a photocopier.

If you use a canvas or evenweave other than those suggested, divide the number of stitches along the length and width of the chart by the number of threads per inch of the fabric to find the finished size of your carpet in inches. To convert this to millimetres, multiply the final number by 25.4.

Each square on a chart represents one stitch over one thread of the canvas, except for the use of cushion stitch on the Aubusson Carpet (*see* Stitch Glossary, page 175). Where alternative background colours are suggested, refer to the photographs of the completed items if you are in any doubt.

It is possible to have a design photocopied, in colour, directly onto the canvas. Details of this option are given in Chapter 14 on page 167.

The materials and threads used are all readily available: any good needlework magazine, trade or telephone directory will list mail-order suppliers and retailers. Equivalent colour numbers for the main brands of threads are given, with the nearest alternative listed where an exact match is not possible.

To avoid repetition, any basic instructions for preparation, beginning and finishing are grouped together in the Techniques section of the book. Instructions specific to a particular group of similar items appear with the projects.

Both metric and imperial measurements are given. In any project use either metric or imperial measurements, not a mixture, as the conversions are equivalents only.

The Projects

2 Carpets

During the eighteenth century wooden floors were made from deal, a pale wood which would have been either stained a darker shade or painted. If painted, the floor might also have been stencilled. Stencilling was especially popular in North America, whilst in Britain geometric patterns in bold colours were more common. Solid floors in high-class houses would have been faced with marble, or, in a less wealthy house, with local stone.

Throughout the eighteenth century, and even into the nineteenth, the most common floor coverings were painted, oiled floor cloths. These were made from a heavy canvas fabric which was first painted, then patterned with block prints or stencilled, and finally sealed with oil. It was also popular to paint these cloths to resemble marble, stone, oak boards or even an Oriental carpet. It was not until later in the eighteenth century that quality houses would have been carpeted. Fitted carpets became popular around the middle of the century, made in strips which were then cut to fit and joined.

The most sought-after carpets were imported and were extremely expensive. These woven and tufted carpets came from the Far East, Turkey and Persia, and also from the prestigious carpet and tapestry weaving centres in France. Embroidered carpets were made as substitutes, sometimes by amateur needlewomen. These were worked in cross stitch on a heavy, open canvas.

A more utilitarian floor covering, called ingrain carpet, was used in less important rooms. This was made with a double-layered weave, usually with a simple, small geometric pattern or stripes. In poor households a drugget would cover the floor, if indeed there was any covering at all. A drugget, usually green or brown, would have been made of serge, baize or hair cloth, all resembling a coarse, woollen cloth. A drugget would also have been used in a quality house, placed over a luxury carpet to protect it from spills.

Towards the end of the eighteenth century, the fashion for Chinoiserie (a form of decoration based on a European idea of Chinese art) brought a revival of the use of matting made from cane, rushes or reeds. These were woven into strips 900mm (3ft) wide and sewn together to form a larger piece.

The designs

The carpets are worked on mono, single-thread canvas, which should be mounted in a rectangular embroidery frame. This will reduce the amount of distortion which can occur when working a piece all in one stitch. Any distortion can be rectified by blocking the carpet after the main embroidery has been completed, but before finishing the edges. The blocking process is described in Chapter 16, Finishing Methods.

Preparation for carpets

The measurement given for the piece of canvas required for each carpet allows extra around the edges to facilitate mounting in a small frame. If you are using a larger frame, a larger piece of canvas than that specified will be needed to fit.

Begin by marking out the stitching area with a line of stitches in tacking cotton, following along a straight row of holes. Mark the four outer edges and the centre lines, vertically and horizontally (*see* Figs 2.1 and 13.7).

Once this is done, mount the canvas in a slate frame or stretcher. This process is covered in Chapter 13, Materials and Working Methods.

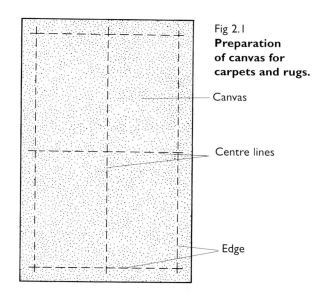

Fig 2.1 **Preparation of canvas for carpets and rugs.**

Canvas

Centre lines

Edge

Working method for carpets

Each carpet has a border pattern enclosing a central design. Either the border or the centre can be worked first – this is simply a matter of choice.

When working the border, I find it easier to begin in the middle of one side and progress towards a corner, following on around the corner and then along the adjacent side towards the next corner (*see* Fig 2.2).

When working the central area, begin with some stitches that are near the centre of the

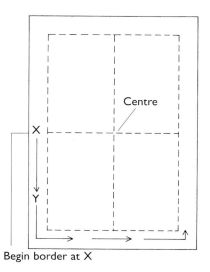

Centre

X

Y

Begin border at X

Fig 2.2 **The best place to start stitching the border.**

carpet. This will make it easier to count from the tacking lines. The tacking lines can be removed when the embroidery approaches them and they are no longer needed.

When working on canvas, always remember to begin with a knot 'in advance'. This process is illustrated in Fig 13.8, Preparation and Beginning.

Often the design requires only two or three stitches in a colour, with a space before the next group of the same colour. There is no need to fasten off each time. Take the thread across the back of the carpet from one group of stitches to the next. Other stitches will gradually cover this thread on the back, and when the final ground colour is worked the back will look reasonably tidy. Work the design details first, and then fill in with the background (*see* Fig 13.9). Fasten off at the back, through the existing stitching.

Finishing hems

Before you begin it is important to bear in mind the method for finishing the hem of the carpet or rug. This involves working the third row of tent stitch in from the edge through the turned hem. It is vital, therefore, not to work this third row until you come to finish the carpet. Remember to block the carpet before finishing the hem if it has distorted as a result of the stitching (*see* Chapter 16).

Working method

1 Trim the excess canvas down to six threads around the edges of the carpet and remove a little canvas from each corner.

2 Fold the corner under diagonally as shown in Fig 2.3, below.

3 Fold each edge under, close to the stitching, to form a mitre at each corner.

4 Now work the remaining row of tent stitch (the third row in) through both layers. The holes in both layers of the canvas should line up.

5 Trim the surplus canvas back to the hem.

6 Leave the carpet under a heavy book or other weight for a couple of days. This will give a good, flat finish. Pressing with an iron can leave an impression of the hem on the right side and is best avoided.

7 A fringe can be added at each end if desired. Chapter 16 explains the method.

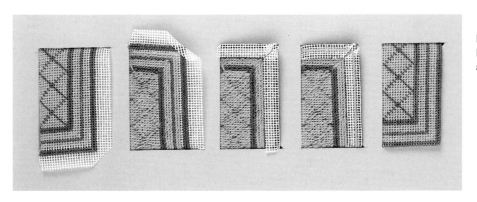

Fig 2.3
**Finishing
a hem.**

Fig 2.4
**Aubusson
carpet.**

Aubusson Carpet

This large floral carpet is based on an eighteenth-century example from the famous Aubusson workshops, which produced quality carpets and tapestries throughout the century. The design features a skeleton cartouche (ornate framework) enclosing a floral spray, surrounded by ribbon-tied floral swags and bouquets. The Rococo influence in this design is especially appropriate for a mid-Georgian setting, but would not be totally out of place in a later house.

Aubusson Carpet

Materials

Mono canvas/Coin net (24 count): 315 x 250mm (12½ x 10in)
OR
Mono canvas (22 count): 355 x 280mm (14 x 11in)
Small rectangular slate frame or stretcher
Stranded cotton as listed in colour key
Tapestry needle: No. 26
Tacking cotton

Size

227 x 166 stitches
Mono canvas/Coin net (24 count): 243 x 177mm (9½ x 7in)
Mono canvas (22 count): 264 x 190mm (10⅜ x 7½in)

11

Fig 2.6 **Chart for Aubusson carpet.**

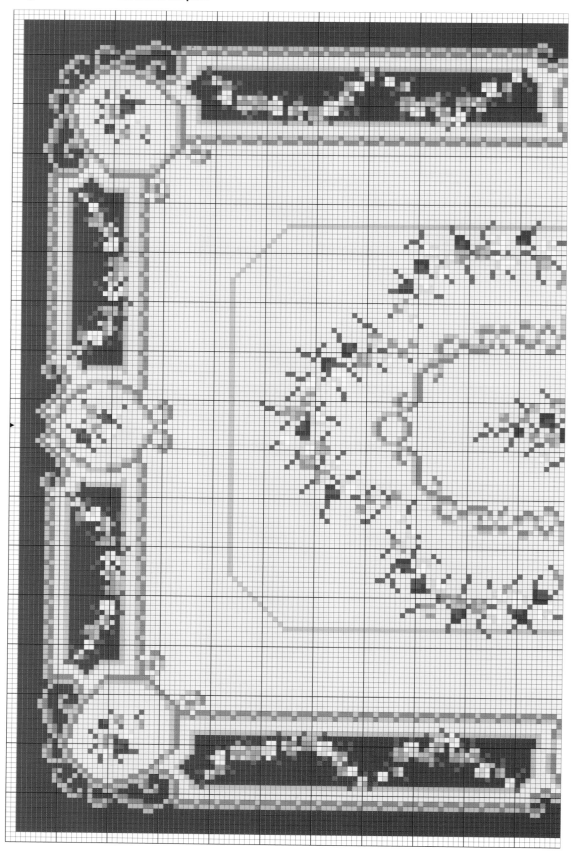

The original woven carpet had a dark madder surround, but a light green or blue also looks well, as Figs 2.4 and 2.5 shows.

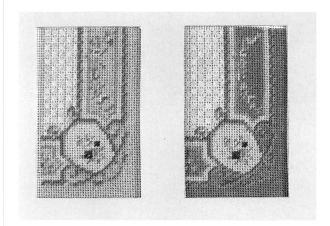

Fig 2.5 **Alternative background colours for the Aubusson carpet.**

Working method

Use two strands of stranded cotton throughout. Prepare the canvas and work the embroidery using the chart in Fig 2.6, following the general instructions given above. Work the centre and outer border in tent stitch, and the background of the inner border in cushion stitch. Cushion stitch gives a chequerboard effect, as shown in Fig 2.4.

When the embroidery has been completed – except for the third row from the edge – remove from the frame. If the canvas has distorted, block it into shape as described in Chapter 16 (*see* page 173).

Finally, turn in and secure the edges by working the third row through both layers as shown in Fig 2.3.

Aubusson Carpet

		Skeins	DMC	Anchor	Madeira
	Gold	1	729	890	2012
	Tan	1	435	1046	2010
	Light peach	1	353	868	0304
	Dark peach	1	352	328	0303
	Light pink	1	818	271	0608
	Dark pink	1	3326	36	0606
	Light red	1	321	47	0510
	Dark red	1	815	43	0512
	Light clover	1	225	1026	0501
	Dark clover	1	223	895	0812
	Green	1	471	255	1502
	Cream	5	677	886	2207

Alternative backgrounds

	Dark red (on chart)	3	815	43	0512
	Light blue	3	809	130	0909
	Light green	3	369	1043	1309

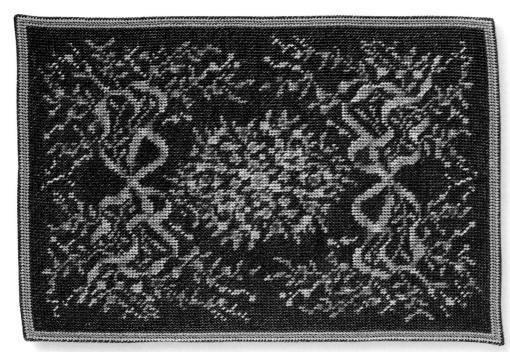

Fig 2.7
**Savonnerie
carpet.**

Savonnerie Carpet

With its multitude of flowers and flowing
ribbons, this design would be suited to any part
of the eighteenth century and to the early years
of the nineteenth.

This design is based on a carpet from the
Savonnerie workshops and shows an elegant
interpretation of the Rococo style. The walnut-
coloured background used here appears on the
original carpet, but any other colour could be
substituted provided it is a strong contrast to
the pinks and yellows of the flowers.

Designs based on the Rococo style were
revived in the early nineteenth century and
became popular motifs for embroidery.

Savonnerie Carpet

Materials

Mono canvas/Coin net (24 count): 250 x 200mm (10 x 8in)
OR
Mono canvas (22 count): 260 x 210mm (10½ x 8½in)
Small rectangular slate frame or stretcher
Stranded cotton as listed in colour key
Tapestry needle: No. 26
Tacking cotton

Size

160 x 112 stitches
Mono canvas/Coin net (24 count): 175 x 126mm (6⅞ x 5in)
Mono canvas (22 count): 195 x 135mm (7⅜ x 5⅜in)

Working method

Use two strands of stranded cotton and tent stitch throughout. Prepare the canvas and work the embroidery, using the chart in Fig 2.8, as described in the general instructions. Begin in the centre of the design. When you have finished the main embroidery – but not the third row – remove it from the frame. If the carpet has distorted, block it back into shape before you complete the hem (*see* Chapter 16).

Complete the hem, as shown in Fig 2.3, by working the third row from the edge through both layers of canvas.

Savonnerie Carpet

		Skeins	DMC	Anchor	Madeira
	Dark pink	1	899	66	0609
	Mid pink	1	776	24	0607
	Light pink	1	225	1026	0501
	Rust	1	355	1014	0401
	Dark peach	1	352	9	0303
	Mid peach	1	353	868	0304
	Light peach	1	754	1012	0305
	Gold	1	676	891	2208
	Yellow	1	3047	886	2205
	Cream	1	951	880	2308
	Dark green	1	3053	859	1059
	Light green	1	369	1043	1309
	Grey green	1	648	900	1902
	Dark blue	1	517	0169	1107
	Mid blue	1	926	850	1707
	Light blue	1	928	274	1708
	Brown	3	839	1050	1913

Fig 2.8 **Chart for Savonnerie carpet.**

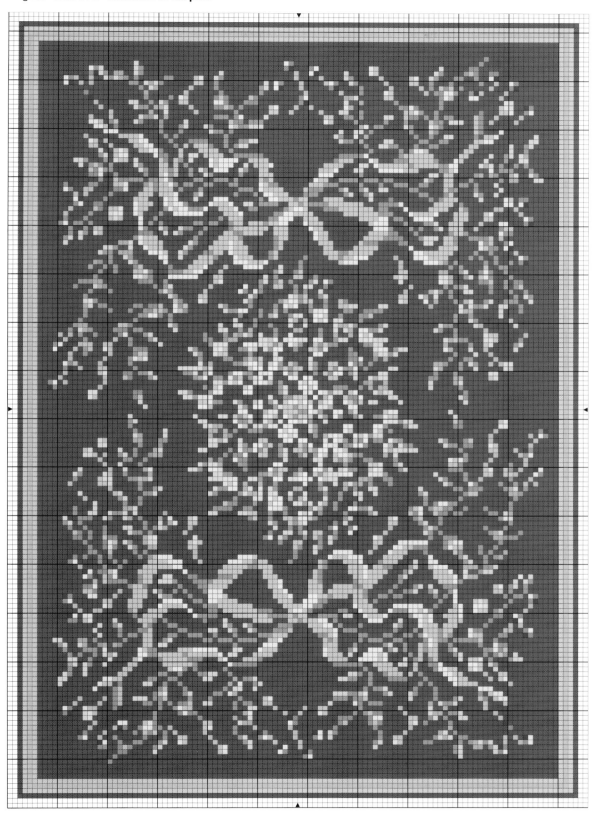

Persian Carpet

Traditional carpet designs from Turkey and Persia were handed down through the generations, and are not confined to one brief period. They usually feature stylized flowers laid out in a geometric way. Background colours are often rich red or blue, contrasted with lighter areas. This carpet could be used throughout the eighteenth and into the nineteenth century.

Fig 2.9 **Chart for Persian carpet.**

Working method

Use two strands of stranded cotton and tent stitch throughout. Prepare the canvas and work the embroidery, using the chart in Fig 2.9, as described in the general instructions. When completed, but before working the third row in from the edge, remove the carpet from the frame. If the piece has distorted, block it back into shape as shown in Chapter 16.

Finally, complete the hem as described on page 10 and shown in Fig 2.3.

Fig 2.10
Persian carpet.

Persian Carpet

Materials

Mono canvas/Coin net (24 count): 320 x 230mm (12½ x 9in)
OR
Mono canvas (22 count): 330 x 250mm (13 x 10in)
Small rectangular slate frame or stretcher
Stranded cotton as listed in colour key
Tapestry needle: No. 26
Tacking cotton

Size

212 x 131 stitches
Mono canvas/Coin net (24 count): 235 x 148mm (9¼ x 5⅞in)
Mono canvas (22 count): 245 x 152mm (9⅝ x 6in)

Persian Carpet

		Skeins	DMC	Anchor	Madeira
	Cream	2	677	886	2207
	Gold	1	729	890	2012
	Orange	1	970	316	0204
	Red	1	817	46	0510
	Pink	1	352	9	0303
	Green	1	730	924	1614
	Blue	2	311	147	1006

Chinese Carpet

Carpets were made in the Far East for export to Europe. The designs reflected the fashion for Chinoiserie, made to European tastes and not resembling true Chinese art. This example is based on an eighteenth-century design from an embroidered hanging, showing a typical tree form with various flowers growing from a little mound.

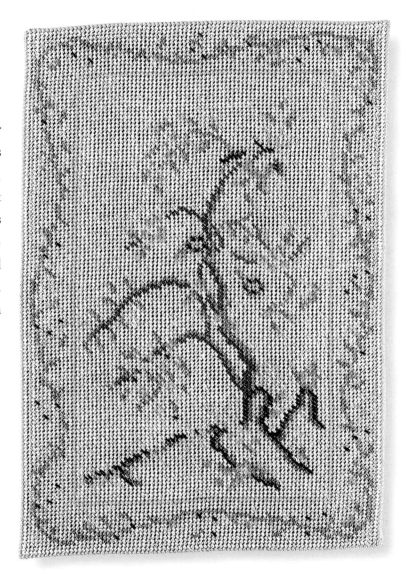

Fig 2.11 **Chinese carpet.**

Chinese Carpet

Materials

Mono canvas/Coin net (24 count): 230 x 180mm (9 x 7in)

OR

Mono canvas (22 count): 240 x 190mm (9½ x 7½in)

Small rectangular slate frame or stretcher

Stranded cotton as listed in colour key

Tapestry needle: No. 26

Tacking cotton

Size

138 x 90 stitches

Mono canvas/Coin net (24 count): 152 x 102mm (6 x 4in)

Mono canvas (22 count): 160 x 105mm (6¼ x 4⅛in)

Working method

Use two strands of stranded cotton and tent stitch throughout. Prepare the canvas and work the embroidery, using the chart in Fig 2.12, as described in the general instructions.

When the embroidery has been completed, but before working the third row in from the edge – remove the carpet from the frame. If the carpet has distorted, block it back into shape as shown in Chapter 16.

Finally, turn the hem and complete the edges by working the third row through both layers of canvas, as shown in Fig 2.3.

Chinese Carpet

		Skeins	DMC	Anchor	Madeira
	Gold	1	725	305	0106
	Caramel	1	435	1046	2010
	Light caramel	1	437	362	2012
	Light gold	1	676	891	2208
	Dark blue	1	311	147	1006
	Mid blue	1	926	850	1707
	Light blue	1	927	849	1708
	Dark peach	1	352	9	0303
	Mid peach	1	353	868	0304
	Light peach	1	951	880	2308
	Dark mushroom	1	839	1050	1913
	Light mushroom	1	841	378	1911
	Dark green	1	502	876	1703
	Light green	1	504	1042	1701
	Light grey	2	762	234	1804

Fig 2.12 **Chart for Chinese carpet.**

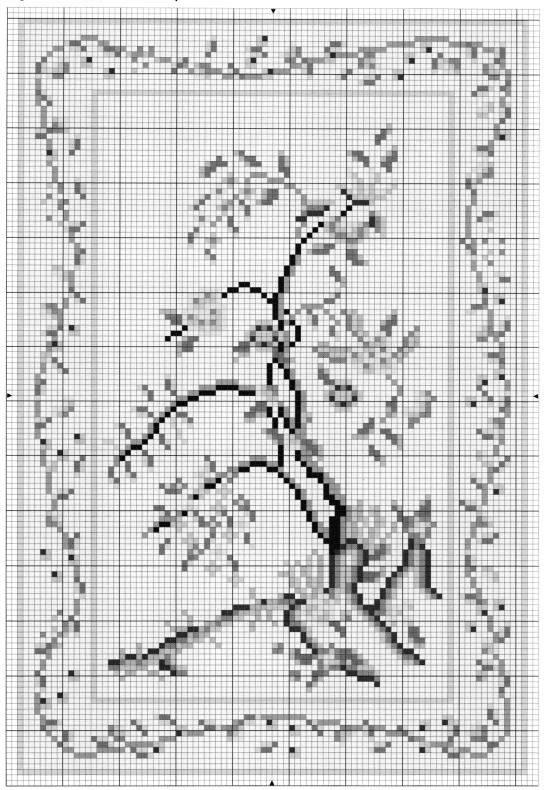

Fig 2.13 **Neo-classical carpet.**

Neo-Classical Carpet

This design features the simpler lines of the Classical Revival of the late eighteenth century, showing a double cartouche and a Greek key motif border. The background colours may be substituted with any two toning shades to suit your decor. A larger version could be made using an 18 count mono canvas.

Working method

Use two strands of stranded cotton on 22 and 24 count, or three strands on 18 count.

Prepare the canvas and work the embroidery, following the chart in Fig 2.14, as described in the general instructions. Begin in the centre and use tent stitch throughout.

When the embroidery has been completed – bar the third row from the edge – remove it from the frame. If it has distorted, block it back into shape as shown in Chapter 16.

Finally, complete the hem by working the third row from the edge through both layers of canvas, as shown in Fig 2.3.

Neo-Classical Carpet

Materials

Mono canvas/Coin net (24 count): 210 x 180mm (8¼ x 7in)
OR Mono canvas (22 count): 220 x 190mm (8½ x 7½in)
OR Mono canvas (18 count): 240 x 200mm (9½ x 8in)
Small rectangular slate frame or stretcher
Stranded cotton as listed in colour key
Tapestry needle: No. 26
Tacking cotton

Size

115 x 81 stitches
Mono canvas/Coin net (24 count): 127 x 92mm (5 x 3⅝in)
Mono canvas (22 count): 133 x 98mm (5¼ x 3⅞in)
Mono canvas (18 count): 162 x 114mm (6⅜ x 4½in)

Neo-Classical Carpet

		Skeins	DMC	Anchor	Madeira
	Gold	1	725	305	0106
	Light blue	1	799	145	0910
	Dark blue	2	820	134	0904

Fig 2.14 **Chart for Neo-classical carpet.**

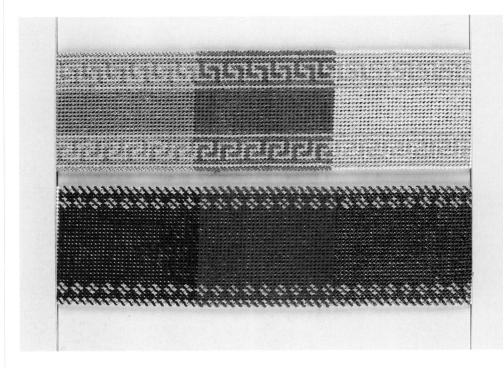

Fig 2.15 **Stair carpet designs. Top: Design 1. Bottom: Design 2.**

Stair carpets

The staircase within a wealthy house was an important feature of an impressive entrance hall, demonstrating to any visitor the status of the owner. In the grandest houses the stairs would have been of stone with wrought-iron balusters. Most houses of the wealthy and middle classes would have been fitted with elegant wooden staircases and slim newel posts with two or three balusters to each stair. Stair carpet was not used until the middle of the eighteenth century, when a carpet or a drugget would sometimes cover a wooden staircase. The grand stone staircases would not have been covered, however.

The two designs shown here feature simple border patterns and would suit a house dated

Stair Carpets

Materials

Mono interlock canvas (18 count): 130mm (5in) x required length + 80mm (3⅛in)

Rectangular slate frame or stretcher

Stranded cotton as listed in colour key (for the background: 1 skein works 190mm (7½in)

Tapestry needle: No. 24

Tacking cotton

Size

32 stitches wide

45mm (1¾in) wide

between 1750 and 1820. The background colour can be altered according to choice. Each sample is shown in three colourways.

When working miniature stair carpet it is best to use interlock canvas. This is a white canvas with a twisted weave, which allows it to be cut to a shape without fraying. This special weave means that interlock canvas is more pliable than regular mono canvas, and it therefore fits into the shape of the stairs more easily.

Width and length

The width of the carpet can be adjusted by adding stitches to the centre of the pattern. The usual width required is 5cm (2in), and a length of 56cm (22in) should fit a standard, straight staircase kit.

To estimate the length of carpet required, cut a strip of paper 5cm (2in) wide and about 60cm (24in) long. Hold one end of the strip against the bottom of the staircase, level with the floor. Carefully fold the rest of the paper into and up each stair until the top stair is reached. Mark this point with a line, then measure the paper strip from the bottom to the line. This will tell you the length of carpet you need to make.

Working method

As with the other carpets, the side edges of the stair carpet are secured by working the third row of stitches through the turned hem, so remember not to work the third row in from each side initially.

Mount the canvas in the frame or stretcher. Mark out the two edges and the required length of the stitching area with tacking stitches.

Use three strands of stranded cotton and tent stitch throughout. Following your preferred chart from Fig 2.16 or 2.17, and referring to the general instructions for carpets, begin with the patterned edges (but not initially the third row) and then fill in the background.

When the carpet is complete, remove it from the frame and check the length on the staircase. If another few rows are needed, these can be worked off the frame.

If necessary, block the canvas as described in Chapter 16. Work the hem as shown in Fig 2.3.

Stair Carpet – Design 1

		Skeins	DMC	Anchor	Madeira
	Gold	1	676	891	2208
Alternative backgrounds					
	Light blue (on chart)	1	813	161	1013
	Rose pink	1	3350	1036	1007
	Light green	1	504	1042	1701

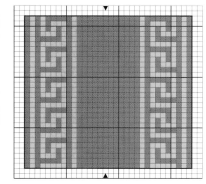

Fig 2.16 **Chart for stair carpet, Design 1.**

Stair Carpet – Design 2

		Skeins	DMC	Anchor	Madeira
	Gold	1	676	891	2208
Alternative backgrounds					
	Mid blue (on chart)	1	824	132	1010
	Red	1	815	43	0512
	Dark green	1	937	268	1504

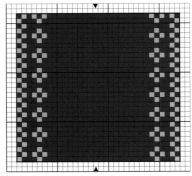

Fig 2.17 **Chart for stair carpet, Design 2.**

Fitting a stair carpet

To fit the completed stair carpet, either use miniature stair rods and follow the maker's instructions, or use the following method. If you are following the steps below, do not try to hurry. Deal with one stair at a time, allowing the glue to dry completely before you move on. This will give the best result, with the carpet fitting flat to each stair.

Working method

1 Fold the lower edge of unworked canvas under and lightly glue into place with PVA.

2 When dry, glue this lower edge to the bottom riser, level with the floor, and leave to dry.

3 Place a line of glue into the rear angle of the first tread (indicated by the arrow in Fig 2.18).

4 Carefully push the stair carpet into the angle using a firm edge. A piece of stiff card or a cut-down credit card would be ideal. Hold it in place until the glue 'grips' and allow to dry completely before proceeding to the next stair.

5 Repeat the process for each individual stair.

6 Turn the unworked canvas under at the top and glue as in step 1.

7 Secure the carpet to the top step or landing as appropriate.

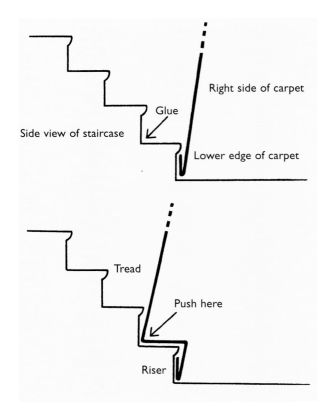

Fig 2.18 **Fitting the stair carpet.**

Photocopying onto fabric

It is possible to have a colour photocopy of a design made directly onto fabric, and this method is particularly suited to carpets and rugs.

You will need to consult the operator at the copy shop as to whether their particular machines have any limitations on fabric type. The results are very good on canvas, and the printed pattern can then be stitched. Evenweave linen or cotton are also successful. The fabric can be embroidered or used with just the photocopied image.

It is essential to ensure that the original picture of the carpet and the fabric are lined up accurately so that the copy appears on the straight grain of the fabric.

Finishing photocopied carpets

Evenweave

Trim the fabric away along the two side edges of the carpet to a 6mm (¼in) turning, fold the edges under and secure with a little fabric glue.

Then trim the fabric away from the two ends of the carpet to between 6 and 10mm (¼ – ⅜in), i.e., the length of the desired fringe. Fray the ends of the carpet until you reach the edge of the copied design.

Canvas

Trim and turn under all four edges and glue in place, or use the method given for hemming carpets on page 10. Make and add a fringe if desired (*see* Chapter 16).

3 Rugs

Being smaller than carpets, rugs were often used in the less prestigious rooms of upper-class houses during the Georgian period. The projects featured here would also suit dolls' houses with rooms which are too small for some of the larger carpet projects included in Chapter 2.

Working methods for rugs

The methods of preparing the canvas, stitching the designs and finishing the hems of rugs are the same as for the carpet projects (*see* pages 9 and 10). Remember not to work the third row of stitches in from the edges initially, as this row forms part of the hem.

Flower and Fruit Rug

The design for this piece is based on an embroidered rug dated c.1750. The original, which is in the Brooklyn Museum in New York, is thought to have been worked by an amateur needlewoman. The red background could be substituted with any other colour to contrast those used for the design.

Fig 3.1 **Flower and Fruit rug.**

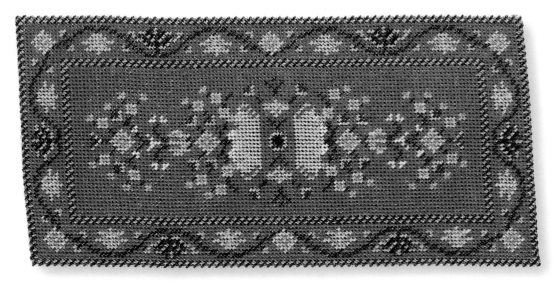

Flower and Fruit Rug

Materials

Mono canvas/Coin net (24 count): 225 x 150mm (9 x 6in)

OR

Mono canvas (22 count): 240 x 160mm (9½ x 6¼in)

Small rectangular frame or stretcher

Stranded cotton as listed in colour key

Tapestry needle: No. 26

Tacking cotton

Size

139 x 69 stitches

Mono canvas/Coin net (24 count): 154 x 78mm (6⅛ x 3¹⁄₁₆in)

Mono canvas (22 count): 162 x 80mm (6⅜ x 3⅛in)

Working method

Use two strands of stranded cotton and tent stitch throughout. Prepare the canvas and work the embroidery, using the chart in Fig 3.2, following the general instructions given for carpets on pages 9 and 10. Begin either in the centre or with the border, whichever you prefer.

When the embroidery has been completed – bar the third row from the edge – remove it from the embroidery frame. If the canvas has distorted, block it back into shape as described in Chapter 16.

Finally, turn under and secure the edges by working the third row of tent stitch through both layers as shown in Fig 2.3 (*see* page 10). A fringe can be added if desired. Instructions for this are given in Chapter 16.

Flower and Fruit Rug

		Skeins	DMC	Anchor	Madeira
	Light green	1	3348	254	1604
	Dark green	1	937	268	1504
	Cream	1	739	1009	2014
	Yellow	1	677	886	2207
	Gold	1	725	305	0106
	Light blue	1	827	9159	1014
	Mid blue	1	798	137	0911
	Dark blue	1	820	134	0904
	Light peach	1	754	1012	0305
	Mid peach	1	353	868	0304
	Dark peach	1	352	9	0303
	Red	2	900	332	0207

Fig 3.2 **Chart for Flower and Fruit rug.**

Fig 3.3 **Flower Basket rug.**

Flower Basket Rug

This design is based on an eighteenth-century embroidered rug which shows the typical mix of influences popular with contemporary designers. The flowers reflect the

Flower Basket Rug

Materials

Mono canvas/Coin net (24 count): 200 x 150mm (8 x 6in)

OR

Mono canvas (22 count): 210 x 160mm (8½ x 6½in)

Small rectangular frame or stretcher

Stranded cotton as listed in colour key

Tapestry needle: No. 26

Tacking cotton

Size

112 x 68 stitches

Mono canvas/Coin net (24 count): 120 x 71mm (4¾ x 2¾in)

Mono canvas (22 count): 128 x 77mm (5 x 3in)

Flower Basket Rug

		Skeins	DMC	Anchor	Madeira
	Dark blue	1	798	137	0911
	Light blue	1	827	9159	1014
	Gold	1	725	305	0106
	Cream	1	738	942	2013
	Dark green	1	937	268	1504
	Light green	1	368	214	1310
	Dark pink	1	899	66	0609
	Light pink	1	225	1026	0501
	Dark red	1	902	897	0601
	Red	1	817	46	0510
	Turquoise	2	747	158	1104

widely admired style of Dutch flower paintings and the basket is standing on a Chinese-style table. The original rug was worked in cross stitch. The pale turquoise background could be substituted with another colour if desired.

Fig 3.4 **Chart for Flower Basket rug.**

Working method

Use two strands of stranded cotton and tent stitch throughout. Following the chart given in Fig 3.4, begin in the centre and work as for the Flower and Fruit rug.

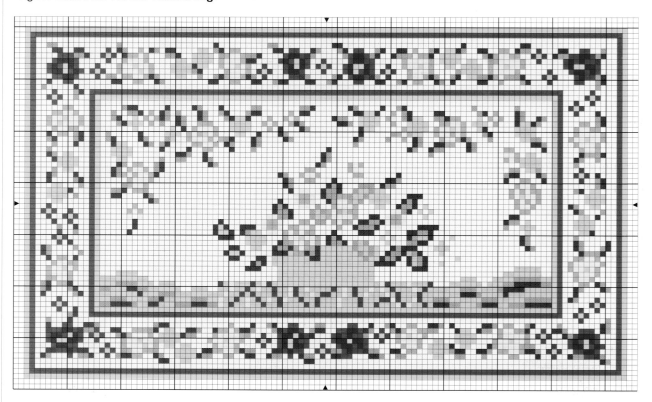

Fig 3.5 **Kashgai rug.**

Kashgai Rug

The design for this rug has been adapted from a Kashgai carpet made at the beginning of the nineteenth century and is typical of the colours used by the nomads of Southern Persia. This rug would suit a late-Georgian dolls' house.

Kashgai Rug

Materials

Mono canvas/Coin net (24 count): 200 x 140mm (8 x 5½in)

OR

Mono canvas (22 count): 210 x 150mm (8½ x 6in)

Small rectangular frame or stretcher

Stranded cotton as listed in colour key

Tapestry needle: No. 26

Tacking cotton

Size

117 x 61 stitches

Mono canvas/Coin net (24 count): 127 x 63mm (5 x 2½in)

Mono canvas (22 count): 134 x 69mm (5¼ x 2¾in)

Working method

Use two strands of stranded cotton and tent stitch throughout. Following the chart in Fig 3.6, begin either in the centre or with the border and work as for the Flower and Fruit rug.

Kashgai Rug

		Skeins	DMC	Anchor	Madeira
	Gold	1	729	890	2012
	Green	1	734	280	1610
	Turquoise	1	597	168	1110
	Orange	1	970	316	0204
	Dark terracotta	1	356	1013	0402
	Light terracotta	1	407	914	2312
	Black	1	310	Black	Black
	Cream	1	Ecru	926	Ecru

Fig 3.6 **Chart for Kashgai rug.**

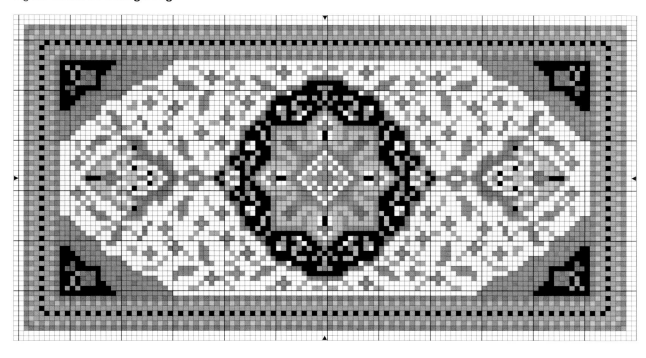

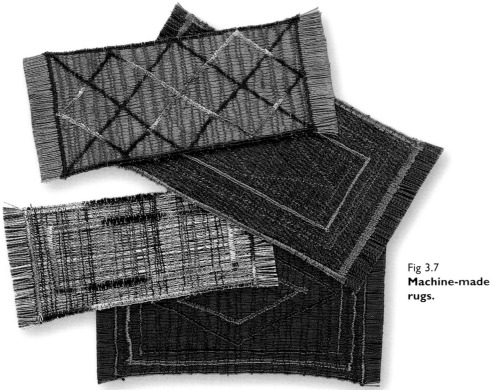

Fig 3.7
**Machine-made
rugs.**

Machine-
made rugs

Small rugs with very simple geometric designs
can be made using a sewing machine. Such
simple designs would be suited to a house of
any period. The examples shown in Fig 3.7 have
been made with plain or random-dyed rayon
machine embroidery threads. Any fine, smooth
threads can be used.

Machine-Made Rugs

Materials	Size
Firm cardboard (mounting board is ideal)	As required
Craft knife	
Cutting board	
Polyester sewing threads OR	
Rayon machine embroidery threads	
Bond-a-web	

Working method

1 Make a card frame as shown in Fig 3.8. This
must not exceed 200 x 150mm (8 x 6in) if it is
to be used successfully with a sewing machine.

2 Cut out the centre with a craft knife,
making the window 15mm (½in) wider and
longer than the intended size of the rug.

3 Mark the centre of each side, and the length
and width of the rug.

4 Cut a notch at one end to secure the end of
the thread (*see* Fig 3.8).

5 Leaving the thread on the reel, secure the
end into the notch, and begin to bind the thread
lengthways around the card frame, keeping
within the two marks indicating the width of
the rug (*see* Fig 3.9, top). Make sure that the
threads lie flat, side by side.

6 When complete, secure the end of the
thread in the notch and cut from the reel.

7 Cut a piece of Bond-a-web to the finished

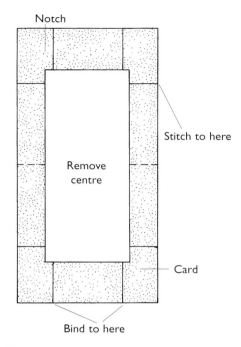

Fig 3.8 **Making and marking the card frame for machine-made rugs.**

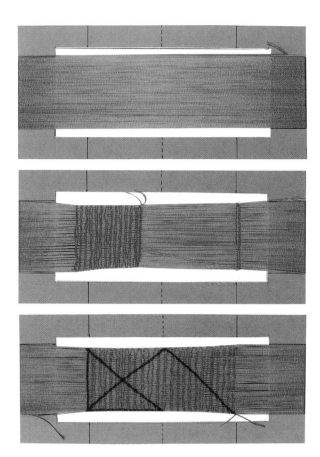

Fig 3.9 **Stages in working the machine-made rugs.**

size of the rug and iron onto the reverse side of the bound threads, within the two marks indicating the length of the rug.

8 With the sewing machine set to a straight stitch of medium length, stitch back and forth across each end of the rug.

9 Continue to stitch back and forth across the rug until the whole area is covered (*see* Fig 3.9, middle). Tie off the ends of the thread.

10 You now have a 'fabric' on which to work the design. For simple patterns, set the machine to a zig-zag stitch of medium width and short length, to give a satin stitch effect (*see* Fig 3.9, bottom). Geometric patterns work well but, with practice, more complicated designs can be achieved. Carefully machine your design into the 'fabric' using various colours as desired. Tie off the ends when complete.

11 To remove the rug from the card frame, cut across the threads at each end, 6–10mm (¼–⅜in) away from the machining to give a fringe.

37

4 Curtains

Curtains were used more in the eighteenth century than in previous times, although folding window shutters were still common.

With the increase in trade, fabrics became more plentiful: printed cotton chintz was imported from India and woven silks were widely available to those who could afford them. During the early Georgian period, very few heavy fabrics were used for curtains or blinds. The main function of covering a window was to exclude sufficient light to protect interior decorations and furnishings. Lightweight, sheer fabrics were used for festoon blinds, which were pulled up and gathered vertically. Alternatively, a sash curtain was used – a fabric blind set into a frame which would fit inside the window recess.

The 1760s saw the rise of the Neo-classical style, influenced by the work of Robert Adam. This style was reflected in the use of curtains in soft, light colours in silk and damask fabrics, or brocatelles with dainty, floral patterns. Richer colours were to be found in the popular watered taffetas in royal blue, turquoise and

Fig 4.1 **Arrangement of draped curtains with tails and tie-backs.**

Fig 4.2 **Alternative variations of draped curtains and tails.**

violet. Pelmets either had inserts of embroidery or were decorated with ornate plasterwork. Such plasterwork can be simulated in miniature by gluing on small pieces of lace and then painting and gilding the resulting 'carving'.

The influence of Chippendale's interior design was to be seen in curtains that overlapped in the centre, with a generous drape secured with tie-backs.

From the 1770s venetian blinds were in use, and the decade also saw the introduction of 'tailed' or 'reefed' curtains. Tailed curtains had drawstrings that gathered the fabric diagonally up and apart, from the centre, so that the outer edges hung down in points.

A wide variety of curtain arrangements remained in use for the rest of the Georgian period, becoming especially ornate in the grander houses. Up to three drapes were hung from the pelmet, with tails to each side, often with the addition of elaborate fringes and tassels.

The designs

The various elements of curtain arrangements included below can be made and arranged according to individual requirements. The first step is to determine the necessary sizes.

Positioning and sizing

1 The hanging rail or top of a pelmet should be placed at least 10mm (⅜in) above the window opening and should extend at least 10mm (⅜in) either side of the opening (*see* A in Fig 4.3).

2 When a full-length curtain is required, take the measurement from the top of the pelmet or rail down to floor level (*see* B in Fig 4.3).

3 For a curtain reaching only to the sill, measure from the top of the pelmet or rail to about 10–15mm (⅜–½in) below the window opening (*see* C in Fig 4.3).

4 As a general guide, the width of each unmade curtain should be at least three times the finished gathered width, with an additional 10mm (⅜in) for the turnings on each side.

Fig 4.3 **Measuring the window for the correct size of curtains and pelmets.**

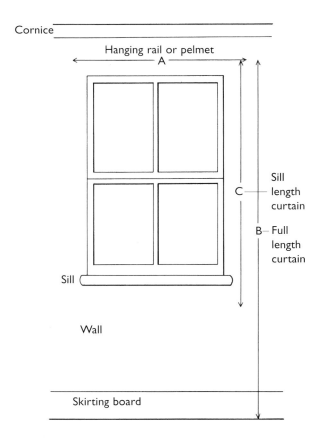

39

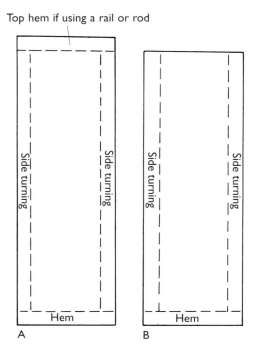

Top hem if using a rail or rod

Side turning Side turning Side turning Side turning

Hem Hem

A B

Fig 4.4 Cutting diagrams for curtains to hang from a pole (A) and curtains for use with a pelmet (B).

5 If the curtains are to hang from a rail with rings, a turning of 10mm (⅜in) is also required at both the top and the hem (*see* A in Fig 4.4). However, if a pelmet is to be used, the allowance at the top is not needed (*see* B in Fig 4.4).

Pleating

There are two ways to pleat the fabric for hanging curtains: gathering by hand or using a commercial pleater (a pliable plastic sheet with regular slots running down from top to bottom). The gathering method allows the pleats to be varied slightly, therefore giving a less rigid effect than the pleater.

The gathering method

1 Cut the fabric to size, including any hem or seam allowances.

2 Turn and stitch or glue any hems. If you are using a PVA fabric glue, use it very sparingly.

3 Turn and stitch or glue the side turnings.

4 On the reverse of the fabric, mark a grid of dots with a soluble fabric pen or dressmakers' carbon (*see* Fig 4.5). The vertical row of dots must align, with about 20mm (¾in) between each dot. The dots can be placed slightly irregularly across the horizontal rows in order to vary the size of the pleats if desired.

5 Thread a needle with polyester sewing

Curtains

Materials

The most suitable fabrics for miniature curtains are lightweight cotton and silk. Fabrics woven with natural fibres drape and pleat more successfully than synthetic fibres. As a general guide, a piece 500mm (20in) square is sufficient to make a pair of curtains with drapes and tails.

Sewing thread to match fabric OR

Fabric glue

Tacking cotton

Embroidery or quilting needle: No. 10

Size

As required

Fig 4.5 **Marking a curtain for gathering.**

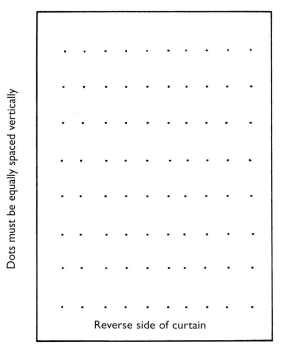

Dots must be equally spaced vertically

Reverse side of curtain

thread and fasten on with a double stitch. Pick up a tiny stitch at each dot, working horizontally across the curtain. Leave the end of the thread free at the end of each row (*see* Fig 4.6).

6 When all the gathering threads are in place, draw up each row and fasten off the threads. As each row is gathered, stroke a needle down the pleat to remove any wrinkles.

7 When all the rows are gathered and fastened off, hold the pleated fabric in front of a steam iron and allow the steam to penetrate the pleats. Use tongs to protect your fingers.

8 Leave the fabric gathered until thoroughly dry. The longer it is left gathered, the better.

9 Gently unfasten each end of the gathering threads and remove them.

Using a commercial pleater

1 Cut out the curtain fabric and turn and secure any hems and side seams as in steps 1, 2 and 3 above.

2 Dampen the fabric slightly and lay it on the pleater, with the slots running vertically down the curtain. Using one of the cards provided, push the fabric down into the first slot.

3 Leaving this card in the slot, push the fabric into the next slot with the second card (*see* Fig 4.7).

Fig 4.6 **Gathering method.**

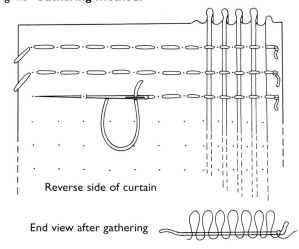

Reverse side of curtain

End view after gathering

Fig 4.7 **Using a pleater.**

Cards

Damp fabric

Pleater

4 Leaving the second card in place, remove the first card and use it to push the fabric into the third slot.

5 Continue in this way until the whole curtain has been fitted into the pleater.

6 Hold a steam iron over the pleater, without actually touching the fabric, and set with a jet of steam.

7 Bond a narrow strip of Bond-a-web along the top edge of the curtain.

8 Leave to dry completely before gently easing the fabric out of the pleater by the bonded strip at the top.

Pelmets

Working method

1 Two basic pelmet patterns are given below. Copy the desired pattern onto stiff card. The length can be adjusted in the centre.

2 Cut out the complete shape using a sharp craft knife and a metal ruler. Score along the broken lines so that the card will fold sharply. Curves and shaped areas can be smoothed and finished with sandpaper or an emery board.

3 To cover the card, cut the fabric for the pelmet at least 10mm (⅜in) larger all round than the card shape (*see* Fig 4.9). Apply Bond-a-web to the reverse side of the fabric.

4 Lay a sheet of non-stick baking parchment on the work surface and, using an iron, bond the fabric to the front of the card. The parchment will prevent the surplus fabric from sticking to the work surface.

5 Fold the turnings over to the reverse side of the pelmet and gently bond into place, trimming or snipping into any corners or shaped edges as you go to allow the turnings to lie flat (*see* Fig 4.9).

Fig 4.8 **Patterns for pelmets. The length can be adjusted at the centre, and the shape of the lower edge can be varied as desired.**

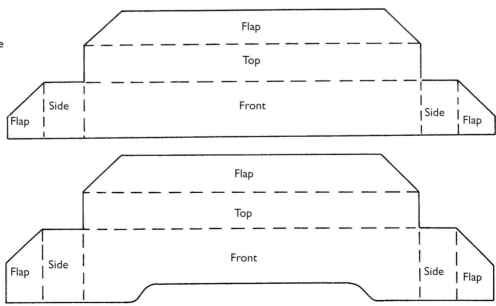

Fig 4.9 **Covering the pelmet.**

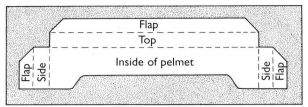

Reverse of fabric with Bond-a-web

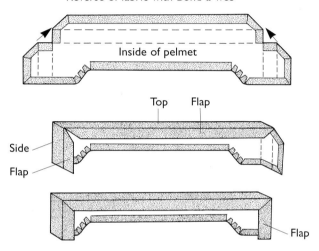

6 Add any braid or trimmings at this stage, using a little fabric glue.

7 Fold back the side and top flaps along the scored lines.

8 When the curtains and any drapes or tails are ready, glue them into position on the inside of the pelmet front, and then fold down the rear flaps of the pelmet and glue into position over the window.

Drapes

The curtains shown in Fig 4.1 have a full set of three drapes with side tails and tie-backs. Alternative arrangements are shown in Fig 4.2.

Working method

1 Make and cover the pelmet following the instructions given above.

2 Trace off the pattern for a drape from Fig 4.10. Cut the number of drapes required,

Fig 4.10 **Pattern for a drape.**

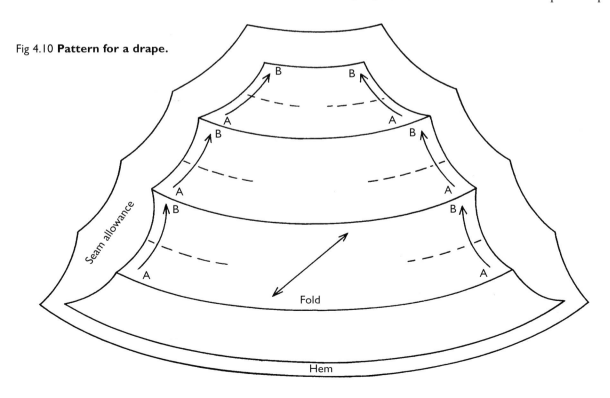

making sure that the fabric is cut on the cross grain, indicated on the pattern by the double-headed arrow.

3 Turn and secure the lower hem by sewing or gluing with fabric glue, and trim with braid if desired. Use the glue very sparingly.

4 Fold the pleats (indicated by the solid and dotted lines) so that A and B meet, and secure them with a small stitch to hold.

5 When the required number of drapes have been made, position and fix them into the pelmet as shown in Fig 4.11.

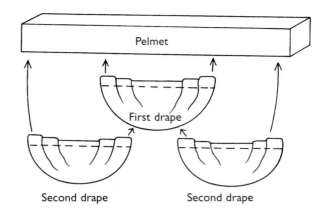

Fig 4.11 **Placing the drapes within the pelmet.**

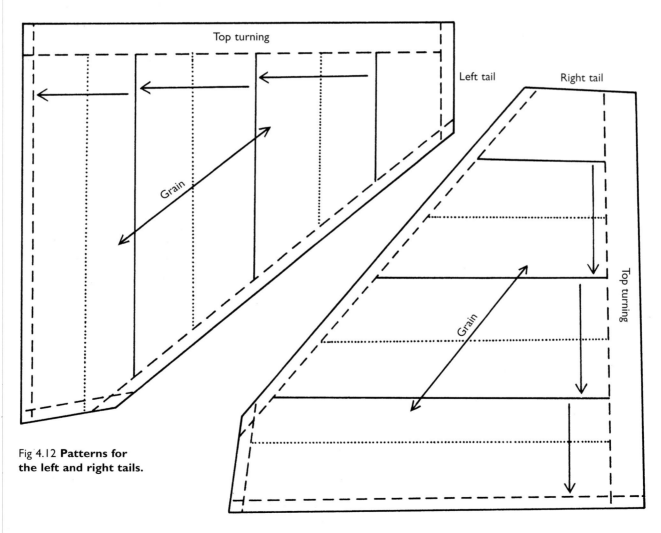

Fig 4.12 **Patterns for the left and right tails.**

Tails

Working method

1 Trace the patterns from Fig 4.12 for a right and left tail. Cut one of each, on the cross grain, from both fabric and lining.

2 Place each pair of curtain fabric and lining right sides together and stitch each one along three sides, as indicated in Fig 4.13.

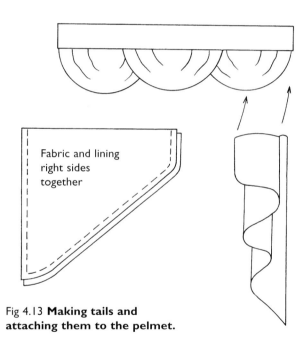

Fabric and lining right sides together

Fig 4.13 Making tails and attaching them to the pelmet.

3 Turn through to the right side and press. Trim with braid if desired.

4 Fold along the pleats as indicated on the pattern (the solid and dotted lines in Fig 4.12). Press lightly with an iron, or leave under a book for softer pleats.

5 Glue the top edges into the pelmet behind the drapes, as indicated in Fig 4.13.

6 Glue the main hanging curtains into place behind the drapes and tails.

Tie-backs

Curtains can be held with either tie-backs or cords and tassels. Cords can be bought, or made from plaited or twisted lengths of thread. (For tassels, *see* Chapter 16.)

Working method

1 Cut one piece of fabric and one of lining, about 100mm (4in) square, and bond together using Bond-a-web.

2 Trace the pattern from Fig 4.14, and make sure the tie-back is long enough to fold around the gathered curtains. The pattern can be lengthened at the centre if required.

Fig 4.14 **Pattern for a tie-back.**

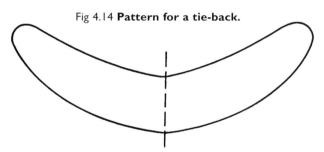

3 Cut the bonded fabric to the exact size of the pattern. No turning is needed.

4 Trim with braid, using either stitching or fabric glue to secure it. Use the glue very sparingly.

5 To fit the tie-back, make a small loop of thread at each end, fold the tie-back around the curtain and hook it onto a small pin which has been fixed to the wall.

OR

Thread a small bead onto a fine pin, fold the tie-back around the curtain and push the pin through both ends of the tie-back. Cut the pin down in length and push it into a small hole in the wall, securing with a tiny spot of glue.

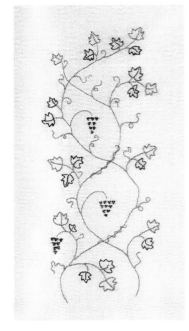

Fig 4.15 Far left
**Crewel work
curtains.**

Fig 4.16 Left
**Crewel work
design.**

Crewel Work Curtains

The design used for this project is based on a set of bed curtains dated between the late seventeenth and early eighteenth century. By this time the heavy, exotic crewel work designs of the seventeenth century had given way to a much lighter form, vines and grapes being a very popular source for the designs (*see* Fig 4.16). These particular curtains look good hanging from a rail, which could be ready-made with rings, or home-made from a piece of brass rod or painted dowelling with beads on each end.

Preparation

Do not initially cut the curtains to size, as the embroidery is best worked in an embroidery frame or stretcher. Mark the outline of the curtain on the fabric with tacking stitches. The measurement will depend on the size of your particular windows

Crewel Work Curtains

Materials

Select a very lightweight cotton or fine silk, as these fabrics will gather and pleat satisfactorily. For each pair, approximately 300mm (12in) square will be needed.

Sewing cotton to match OR
Fabric glue
Stranded cotton as listed in colour key
Embroidery or quilting needle: No. 10

Size

As required

(*see* page 39). The average width of a curtain is about 75mm (3in) for each of a pair.

Using the pattern from Fig 4.17, transfer the design onto the fabric by tracing through with a soluble fabric pen or fabric pencil. A lightweight fabric will usually allow the design to be seen through it. Alternatively, the fabric can be fixed to a window with masking tape, with the

Fig 4.17 **Pattern for crewel work curtain.**

design behind it. The window acts like a light-box, allowing the design to be traced easily. A speedier method is to photocopy the design and iron the copy onto the fabric. However, this method does reverse the design. Full details of all these methods are given in Chapter 14.

Working method

Work the embroidery, using the coloured stitch diagram in Fig 4.18 as a guide. Use one strand

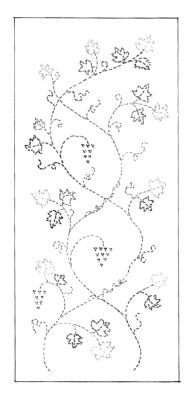

Fig 4.18 **Stitch pattern for crewel work curtain.**

Crewel Work Curtain

		Skeins	DMC	Anchor	Madeira
	Dark green	1	319	683	1313
	Mid green	1	904	258	1413
	Light green	1	906	256	1410
	Mauve	1	3041	871	0806
	Brown	1	612	888	2108

of stranded cotton throughout. The grapes are worked in French knots and the rest of the design in backstitch.

When the embroidery is complete, turn in any hems as directed in the general instructions on pages 39 and 40. Gather or pleat the fabric as described earlier (*see* pages 40–2). Stitch miniature curtain rings along the top edge of each curtain and hang from the rail. Fix the rail to the wall with small eyelet rings.

This pattern can also be used for a wall hanging instead of a curtain.

Fig 4.19 **A gathered blind.**

Window Blinds

Gathered blinds, also called festoon blinds, were often used in Georgian times as efficient ways to exclude light. They could be adjusted vertically by cords to vary the length.

Working method

1 Make a pattern from paper, following Fig 4.20.

A–B = 3 × width of window + 5mm (¼in) turning on each side.

B–C = 2 × height of window + 15mm (½in) for top hem and 5mm (¼in) for lower hem.

2 Use the pattern to cut out the fabric either on the straight grain or the cross grain (*see* Materials panel).

3 Fold back the lower hem and either glue or stitch it in place.

4 Make a stitched hem at the top. This hem will be used to hold a metal rod or piece of dowelling from which the blind will hang.

5 Fold back the two side turnings, securing with a gathering thread.

6 Run a gathering thread along the inner two broken lines (*see* Fig 4.20).

7 Gently gather the four vertical gathering threads until the required depth of blind is achieved, then fasten off the ends.

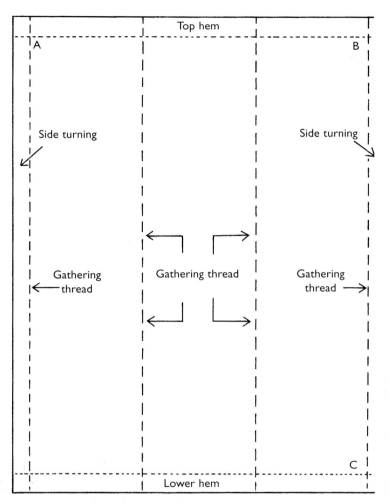

Fig 4.20 **Pattern for gathered blind.**

8 Insert a metal rod or piece of $\frac{1}{16}$in or $\frac{3}{32}$in dowelling into the top hem and push the fabric into folds until the blind fits the width of the window. Arrange the gathers into evenly draped sections (*see* Fig 4.19).

9 Place a bead on each end of the rod and then fix it to the wall, over the window, with eyelet rings or glue.

Window Blinds

Materials

For miniature blinds, very lightweight fabrics should be used, e.g. muslin, silk, cotton lawn or voile. The amount required will depend on the size of the window. For each blind you will need a piece of fabric three times the width of the window plus 10mm ($\frac{3}{8}$in) and twice the height of the window plus 20mm ($\frac{3}{4}$in). Muslin and voile can be cut on the straight grain, whereas silk or cotton lawn are best cut on the cross grain which will require more fabric.

Polyester sewing thread

PVA fabric glue

Fine sewing needle

Size

As required

5 Cushions, chair covers and footstools

Embroidered and canvaswork cushions were used throughout the Georgian period for both comfort and decoration. Canvaswork was an extremely popular choice for embroiderers as it proved to be very durable. The designs for the projects in this chapter are based on eighteenth-century examples in museums and private collections.

Fig 5.1 **Canvaswork cushions.**

Canvaswork cushions

Of the six canvaswork cushions included here, four are worked on canvas and two are worked on evenweave linen to give a more detailed design. Silk gauze can be substituted for the linen, but the gauze is rather more difficult to obtain.

Canvas Cushions

The four designs, worked on 22 count canvas, show various floral themes – the most popular design source in Georgian times. In earlier centuries flowers and plants were often shown growing from a grassy mound or as a 'tree of life'. In the eighteenth century flowers were depicted in ornate vases and urns, tied with ribbons, or tumbling from a cornucopia.

Canvas Cushions

Materials

For each cushion

Mono canvas (22 count): 100mm (4in) square

Stranded cotton as listed in colour key

Lightweight fabric for back of cushion to match background colour: 100mm (4in) square

Filling material (*see* Filling Cushions, page 64)

Tapestry needle: No. 24 or 26

Size

Designs 1, 2 and 3

33 x 33 stitches

38 x 38mm (1½ x 1½in)

Design 4

27 x 44 stitches

30 x 50mm (1⅟₁₆ x 2in)

Fig 5.2 **Floral cushion, Design 1.**

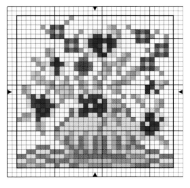

Fig 5.3 **Chart for Floral cushion, Design 1.**

Floral Cushion – Design 1

		Skeins	DMC	Anchor	Madeira
	Dark red	1	816	1005	0512
	Red	1	321	47	0510
	Peach	1	950	376	2309
	Yellow	1	743	305	0113
	Gold	1	729	890	2012
	Light blue	1	813	161	1013
	Blue	1	798	137	0911
	Dark green	1	470	266	1410
	Light green	1	472	264	1414
	Dark grey green	1	502	876	1703
	Light grey green	1	504	1042	1701
	Ecru	1	Ecru	926	Ecru

Design 1

Follow Figs 5.2 and 5.3. This is based on a small picture c.1700–50, showing the flowers arranged in a vase in the style of the Dutch painters.

Fig 5.4 **Floral cushion, Design 2.**

Fig 5.5 **Chart for Floral cushion, Design 2.**

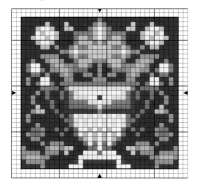

Floral Cushion – Design 2

		Skeins	DMC	Anchor	Madeira
	Dark blue	I	798	137	0911
	Ligbht blue	I	813	161	1013
	Dark pink	I	602	63	0702
	Rose pink	I	899	66	0609
	Light pink	I	776	050	0607
	Ecru	I	Ecru	926	Ecru
	Dark green	I	470	266	1410
	Light green	I	472	264	1414
	Yellow	I	743	305	0113
	Dark red	I	816	1005	0512

Floral Cushion – Design 3

		Skeins	DMC	Anchor	Madeira
	Dark green	I	470	266	1410
	Light green	I	472	264	1414
	Grey green	I	502	876	1703
	Dark blue	I	798	137	0911
	Light blue	I	813	161	1013
	Orange	I	971	316	0203
	Gold	I	729	890	2012
	Yellow	I	743	305	0113
	Peach	I	950	376	2309
	Pink	I	776	050	0607
	Red	I	321	47	0510
	Dark red	I	816	1005	0512
	Black	I	310	403	Black

Fig 5.6 **Floral cushion, Design 3.**   Fig 5.7 **Chart for Floral cushion, Design 3.**

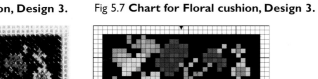

Fig 5.8 **Floral cushion, Design 4.**

Fig 5.9 **Chart for Floral cushion, Design 4.**

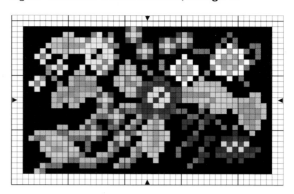

Floral Cushion – Design 4

		Skeins	DMC	Anchor	Madeira
	Dark grey green	I	502	876	1703
	Light green	I	472	264	1414
	Dark green	I	470	266	1410
	Yellow	I	743	305	0113
	Gold	I	729	890	2012
	Dark red	I	816	1005	0512
	Red	I	321	47	0510
	Peach	I	950	376	2309
	Dark pink	I	602	63	0702
	Light pink	I	776	050	0607
	Ecru	I	Ecru	926	Ecru
	Blue	I	798	137	0911
	Tan	I	407	914	2312
	Black	I	310	403	Black

Design 2

Follow Figs 5.4 and 5.5. This reflects the influence of Chinoiserie with a symmetrical arrangement of stylized flowers in an Oriental vase. The original chair seat design is dated 1737.

Design 3

Follow Figs 5.6 and 5.7. Based on a mid-eighteenth-century chair seat, this design is more naturalistic in style, but the blue vase hints at the Oriental influence.

Design 4

Follow Figs 5.8 and 5.9. Being rectangular, this is suited to a bench seat, stool or window seat. This design is based on a mid-eighteenth-century cushion.

Fig 5.10 Serenade cushion.

Fig 5.11 Pastoral Maid cushion.

Evenweave Linen Cushions

The two other cushions shown in Fig 5.1 have been worked on evenweave linen to enable a more detailed design to be stitched. In the examples shown, the linen has been stained with black coffee to give a background colour. Alternatively, a thread colour has been given in the chart key for those who would prefer to work the background in tent stitch.

The 'Serenade' cushion (*see* Figs 5.12 and 5.14) is based on an English settee c.1710 depicting a romantic rural scene, a popular subject seen in contemporary paintings. The 'Pastoral Maid' cushion (*see* Figs 5.13 and 5.15) is based on an embroidered picture by Sarah Warren of Boston, dated 1748.

Working method for canvas and linen cushions

1 If you are using evenweave and you wish it to be coloured, do this first. Instructions are given in Chapter 15.

2 Mount the canvas or evenweave in a small frame or card mount (*see* Chapter 13) and mark the outer edges with a line of tacking stitches or using a fabric pen.

3 Follow your chosen chart, using two strands of stranded cotton on the 22 count canvas, or one strand on the 35 count evenweave.

4 Using tent stitch throughout, work the design first and then fill in the background. On these small items it is sometimes easier to begin at one of the lower corners.

5 When the embroidery is complete, remove it from the frame. If it has distorted, block it into shape (*see* Chapter 16).

6 Make up the cushion as described on page 63, and finish the edges using one of the alternative methods shown on pages 64 and 65.

Evenweave Linen Cushions

Materials

For each cushion

Evenweave linen (35 count): 100 x 200mm (4 x 8in), including cushion back

Stranded cotton as listed in colour key

Filling material (see Filling Cushions, page 64)

Tapestry needle: No. 26

Size

Each cushion

48 x 48 stitches

34 x 34mm (1⅜ x 1⅜in)

Fig 5.12 **Serenade design.**

Fig 5.13 **Pastoral Maid design.**

Evenweave Linen Cushions

		Skeins	DMC	Anchor	Madeira
	Light green	1	472	264	1414
	Mid green	1	470	266	1410
	Dark green	1	319	683	1313
	Red	1	321	47	0510
	Peach	1	948	1011	0306
	Yellow	1	743	305	0113
	Dark brown	1	839	1050	1913
	Light brown	1	3045	888	2103
	Cream	1	677	886	2207

Serenade Cushion only

	Terracotta	1	356	1013	0402
	Light blue	1	799	145	0910
	Grey	1	3072	234	1805

Pastoral Maid Cushion only

	Blue	1	799	145	0910
	White	1	Blanc	White	White

Fig 5.14 **Chart for Serenade cushion.**

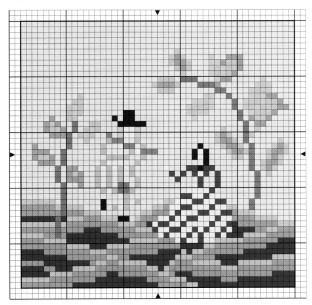

Fig 5.15 **Chart for Pastoral Maid cushion.**

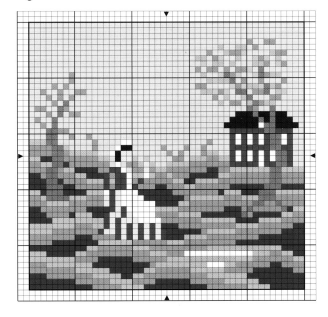

Fig 5.16 **Crewel work cushions. Left to right: Design 1, Design 2, Design 3.**

Embroidered Cushions

Embroidered cushions look best worked on lightweight silk, but soft, fine cotton fabric is a good substitute. Synthetic fabrics can also be used, provided they are soft and pliable.

The three crewel work designs shown in Figs 5.16 and 5.17 are flower sprays adapted from a bedspread dated to the middle of the eighteenth century.

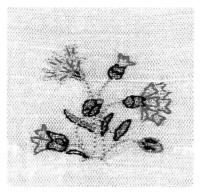
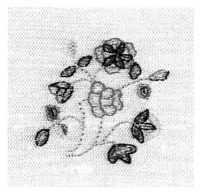

Fig 5.17 **The crewel work designs.**

Embroidered Cushions

Materials

For each cushion

Silk or cotton fabric for front and back of cushions: approx. 100 x 200mm (4 x 8in)

Stranded cotton as listed in colour key

Filling material (*see* Filling Cushions, page 64)

Embroidery or crewel needle: No. 10

Size

Each cushion

38mm (1½in square)

Fig 5.18 **Patterns
for the crewel
work cushions.
Left to right:
Design 1, Design 2,
Design 3 .**

Working method

1   Select the desired pattern from Fig 5.18.

2   Transfer the design (full details are given in Chapter 14) onto the fabric using one of the following methods:

(a) Lay the fabric over the pattern and trace the lines with either a transfer pencil or a water-soluble pen.

(b) Either trace the pattern onto tracing paper with a transfer pencil or photocopy it. Iron off the resulting copy onto the fabric. Remember that both these iron-off methods will reverse the image on the fabric.

3   Mount fabric in a small frame or card mount.

4   Using the relevant coloured stitch diagram as a guide (*see* Figs 5.19, 5.20 and 5.21), work the design with one strand of stranded cotton in backstitch throughout. Design 1 also uses French knots, which are indicated by dots on the diagram.

5   When the embroidery is complete, make up and edge the cushion as shown on pages 63–5.

Fig 5.19 **Stitch pattern for crewel
work cushion, Design 1.**

Crewel Work Cushion – Design 1

		Skeins	DMC	Anchor	Madeira
	Dark blue	1	823	152	1008
	Mid blue	1	798	137	0911
	Light blue	1	827	9159	1014
	Brown	1	612	888	2108
	Yellow	1	725	305	0106
	Gold	1	680	907	2210
	Light green	1	320	216	1311
	Red	1	816	1005	0512
	Pink	1	899	66	0609

Crewel Work Cushion – Design 2

		Skeins	DMC	Anchor	Madeira
	Dark blue	I	823	152	1008
	Brown	I	612	888	2108
	Yellow	I	725	305	0106
	Light green	I	320	216	1311
	Red	I	816	1005	0512
	Pink	I	899	66	0609

Fig 5.20 **Stitch pattern for crewel work cushion, Design 2.**

Fig 5.21 **Stitch pattern for crewel work cushion, Design 3.**

Crewel Work Cushion – Design 3

		Skeins	DMC	Anchor	Madeira
	Dark blue	I	823	152	1008
	Mid blue	I	798	137	0911
	Brown	I	612	888	2108
	Yellow	I	725	305	0106
	Gold	I	680	907	2210
	Light green	I	320	216	1311
	Red	I	816	1005	0512
	Pink	I	899	66	0609

Fig 5.22 **Patchwork cushions.**

Patchwork cushions

Successful miniature patchwork relies largely on the choice of fabric. Very fine cotton with tiny motifs or lightweight, pure silk fabrics are best. Synthetics do not work well as the seams do not press flat enough. Instructions for two simple methods of making pieced miniature patchwork are given below, but simulated patchwork is the best way to achieve the correct scale for more complicated patterns (*see* page 61). Additional designs suited to the Georgian period can be found in my companion volume *Miniature Embroidery for the Victorian Dolls' House.*

Simple Strip Patchwork Cushion

This method can be used with either light-weight, pure cotton or silk fabric.

Working method

1 Begin by tracing or photocopying the pattern from Fig 5.23A.
2 Transfer the pattern onto the square of Habutai silk. The photocopy can be ironed onto the silk, or the tracing placed behind it and drawn on with a transfer pen or pencil. Full details of these methods are given in Chapter 14.
3 Using the lines on the pattern as a guide, place each strip of coloured fabric into position

Simple Strip Patchwork

Materials
For each cushion

Habutai silk (very thin silk lining): 75mm (3in) square

Strips of silk or cotton: 18 x 45mm (¾ x 1¾in) x 12. (These could be 12 different
    colours; 3 colours repeated 4 times; or 4 colours repeated 3 times.)

Additional piece of one of the fabrics: 50mm (2in) square

Size
As required

Fig 5.23 **Assembling strip patchwork cushions.**

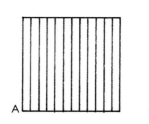
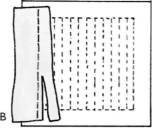
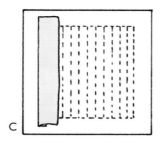
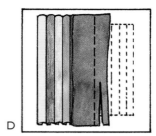

Fig 5.24 **Assembling square patchwork cushions.**

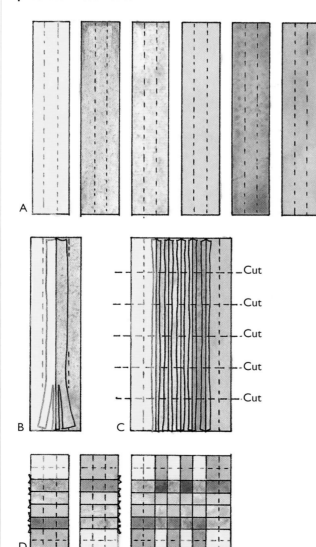

in turn and stitch by machine or hand. This can be done from the back, as the lines on the pattern can be seen through the fine silk.

Trim away some of the turning, then fold over and press each strip before placing the next (*see* Figs 5.23B and C).

4 Continue adding the strips (*see* Fig 5.23D) until all 12 are attached.

5 Make up and edge the cushion as shown on pages 63–5.

Simple Square Patchwork Cushion

Working method

1 Machine stitch the strips together, initially in pairs, allowing a 6mm (¼in) seam on each side. Press the seam open and then trim the seam allowance away (*see* Fig 5.24B). It is easier to press the seam flat before trimming.

2 Continue to machine stitch the strips together, pressing and trimming the turnings, until all six strips are joined (*see* Fig 5.24C).

3 Cut across the strips, as indicated in Fig 5.24C.

4 Arrange the resulting six new strips top to

Simple Square Patchwork

Materials

For each cushion

Lightweight, pure cotton or silk fabric in six co-ordinating colours:

  18 x 108mm (¾ x 4¼in) piece of each colour

Additional piece of one of the fabrics: 50mm (2in) square

Size

As required

tail to alternate the colours (*see* Fig 5.24D). Join these together, by machine or hand, pressing and trimming the seams above. You now have the front of the cushion, with a 6mm (¼in) turning around the edges.

Fig 5.25 **Simulated patchwork cushions.**

5 Make up and edge the cushion as shown on pages 63–5.

Simulated Patchwork Cushion

Very tiny or intricate patchwork designs can be simulated using fabric transfer paints. Detailed instructions for using these are given in Chapter 15. Fabric transfer paints are most suited to synthetic fabrics. Choose a soft, pliable fabric such as crêpe de Chine, crêpe-backed satin or any other lightweight, soft fabric.

Working method

Take a photocopy of the required pattern from Fig 5.26 and use fabric transfer paints to colour the photocopy as desired. The paints can be

Simulated Patchwork

Materials

For each cushion

Suitable fabric: 75 x 150mm (3 x 6in)

Muslin: 75mm (3in) square x 3

Sewing thread to match fabric

Embroidery or quilting needle: No. 10

Fabric transfer paints

Size

As required

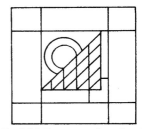 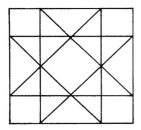

Fig 5.26 **Patterns for simulated patchwork cushions.**

mixed together to create new colours. Leave this to dry. Cut your chosen fabric into two pieces, 75mm (3in) square, to form the front and back of the cushion, then iron the coloured copy onto the fabric for the front of the cushion. It is advisable to have a sheet of paper underneath the fabric to protect the working surface, as the colour may sometimes penetrate through the fabric.

It is possible to use the resulting printed fabric as it is, in which case, make up and edge the cushion as shown on pages 63–5. However, if the piece is quilted lightly, a better impression of patchwork is achieved because the coloured segments of the pattern appear to be joined. To work the quilting, follow the directions given for quilted cushions before making up and edging the cushion.

 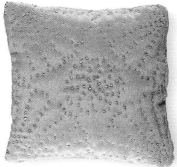 

Fig 5.27 **Quilted cushions.**

Quilted Cushions

Quilting was extremely popular during the eighteenth century, both for furnishings and costume. The designs for the cushions shown in Fig 5.27, based on the feather or fan motif, are suited to the whole Georgian period. Very soft, lightweight fabrics should be used to give the correct feeling of scale. Silk, cotton lawn, crêpe de Chine or crêpe-backed satin are all suitable.

Working method

1 Select and photocopy your chosen design from Fig 5.28.

2 Iron the photocopy onto the Habutai silk backing.

3 Prepare the fabrics by laying the main fabric over the muslin layers or Domette and placing them all onto the Habutai silk with the photocopied pattern showing underneath (*see* Fig 5.29A).

Quilted Cushions

Materials

For each cushion

Main fabric: 100mm (4in) square x 2

Habutai silk or fine cotton lawn: 100mm (4in) square

Muslin: 100mm (4in) square x 4 OR

Domette: 100mm (4in) square

Sewing or quilting thread to match chosen fabric

Quilting needle: No. 10 or 12

Size

As required

Fig 5.28
Patterns for quilted cushions.

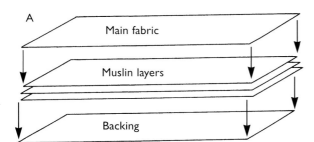

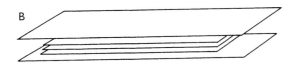

Fig 5.29 **Assembling fabrics for quilting.**

4 Using a matching thread and working from the wrong side (i.e. the Habutai backing with pattern), quilt the layers together with a tiny running stitch, following the lines of the design.

5 When the quilting is complete, trim away some of the surplus muslin or Domette around the edge (*see* Fig 5.29B) and make up and edge the cushion as described below.

Making up the cushions

1 Trim the seam allowances on the front and back of the cushion to a width of about 6mm (¼in) (*see* Fig 5.30A).

2 Turn the edges to the reverse side (*see* Fig 5.30B) and, using a No. 10 embroidery or quilting needle, stitch the front and back of the cushion together, leaving part of one side open.

3 Fill the cushion (*see* below) and complete the stitching to close the opening.

63

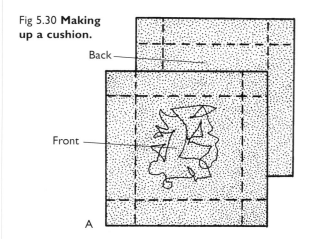

Fig 5.30 **Making up a cushion.**

Back

Front

A

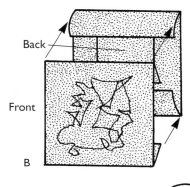

Back

Front

B

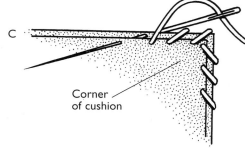

C

Corner
of cushion

Filling cushions

If you require a firmly padded effect, fill the cushion with wadding or kapok. Tease the wadding or kapok out into very small pieces and push these into the cushion, filling the corners first. Make sure that you do not over-stuff the cushion.

For a more 'lived-in' look, fill the cushion about three-quarters full with small plastic or glass beads. When the opening has been stitched closed, the cushion can be pushed gently into the corner of an armchair or settee with a finger, leaving a realistic dent.

Alternative edgings for cushions

A simple edging can be created with an oversewing stitch to join the back and front of the cushion (*see* Fig 5.31A). This can be worked in a contrasting thread if desired.

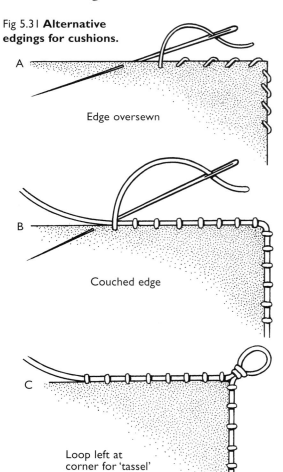

Fig 5.31 **Alternative edgings for cushions.**

A

Edge oversewn

B

Couched edge

C

Loop left at
corner for 'tassel'

Alternatively, a couched thread can be laid to simulate a corded edge. This is especially effective if a contrasting thread is used to stitch the laid thread down (*see* Fig 5.31B).

Using the couching method, a simple tassel can be made by leaving a loop of thread at each corner. The loop is then cut and trimmed to make the 'tassel' (*see* Fig 5.31C).

Fig 5.32 **Chairs fitted with embroidered backs and seats.**

Chair Covers

These projects can be used for chair seats or backs and upholstered armchairs. The first three designs are all-over patterns which can be embroidered to any shape or size to fit ready-made chairs or kits.

If you are using a kit, use the template included as a pattern, allowing extra fabric all round for turnings. For a ready-made chair, take a tracing of the seat or back, add a turning all round and use this as a pattern.

Working method for chair covers

1 Using the template or pattern, mark the outline of the seat or back on the fabric or canvas with a fabric pen, then mark the centre lines, from front to back and across.

2 Work your chosen pattern from the relevant chart, starting from the centre point. Use tent

Chair Covers

Materials
For each chair seat or back

Stranded cotton as listed in colour key

Linen evenweave (35 count): 100mm (4in) square (For an upholstered chair, lay pattern
    pieces out and measure amount of fabric required)

Tapestry needle: No. 24 or 26

Felt, Domette or thin wadding: small quantity

Thin card

Size
As required

Fig 5.33 **Covering a chair seat or back.**

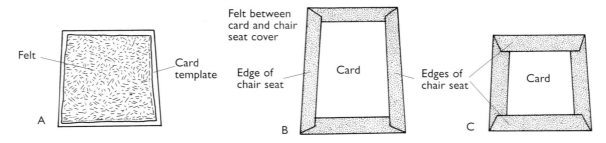

stitch with one strand of stranded cotton throughout. Cover the shape of the chair seat or back with embroidery, taking the stitches a little beyond the outline to allow for any padding.

3 When the embroidery is complete, cut a piece of thin card to the exact size of the seat or back. Cut a piece of felt or thin wadding slightly smaller than the card and fix it onto the card with a spot of glue (*see* Fig 5.33A). Do not be tempted to use too much felt or wadding, as this will spoil the scale of the piece.

4 Place the embroidery over the padded card so that the felt or wadding is in the middle, and take the turnings over the edges to the reverse side. Secure with fabric glue, trimming any excess fabric away (*see* Fig 5.33B and C).

5 Place the prepared seat or back into position on the chair and secure with a little PVA glue.

Fig 5.34 **The three all-over designs: Grape and Vine, Flower Motif and Medallion Florentine.**

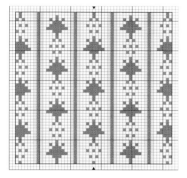

Fig 5.35 **Chart for Grape and Vine chair seat.**

Grape and Vine design

With its pastel stripes this design is particularly suited to the late Georgian or Regency period (*see* Fig 5.34 and the chart in Fig 5.35).

Grape Vine Chair Seat

		Skeins	DMC	Anchor	Madeira
	Mauve	1	3041	871	0806
	Green	1	502	876	1703
	Pink	1	224	893	1813
	Ecru	1	Ecru	926	Ecru

Flower Motif design

This flower design reflects a popular theme through the whole Georgian era. Other colours can be used for the background if desired (*see* Fig 5.34 and the chart in Fig 5.36).

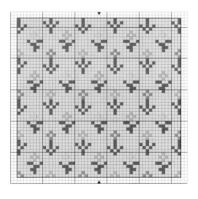

Fig 5.36 **Chart for Flower Motif chair seat.**

Flower Motif Chair Seat

		Skeins	DMC	Anchor	Madeira
	Yellow	1	744	301	0110
	Green	1	320	216	1311
	Pink	1	899	66	0609
	Blue	1	827	9159	1014
	Orange	1	740	316	0202
	Mauve	1	316	1017	0809
Alternative backgrounds					
	Light green (on chart)	1	504	1042	1701
	Ecru	1	Ecru	926	Ecru

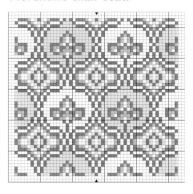

Fig 5.37 **Chart for Medallion Florentine chair seat.**

Medallion Florentine design

This would suit the mid- to late-Georgian period. This can also be worked in a variety of colourways (*see* Fig 5.34 and the chart in Fig 5.37).

Medallion Florentine Chair Seat

		Skeins	DMC	Anchor	Madeira
	Dark green	1	502	876	1703
	Dark pink	1	602	63	0702
	Light pink	1	899	66	0609
	Blue	1	827	9159	1014
	Cream	1	Ecru	926	Ecru

Fig 5.38 **Rose Posy design.**

Rose Posy design

This design can be used for a chair seat or matching seat and back (*see* Fig 5.38 and the chart in Fig 5.39). It is also shown later in the book as a pole screen and part of a set of bed hangings (*see* pages 111 and 112). The simple posy tied with ribbon is typical of many motifs used throughout the Georgian period. In the example shown, the white background linen has been coloured with black coffee to give an antique effect. The linen could also be coloured with a fabric dye. Full details on colouring fabric are given in Chapter 15.

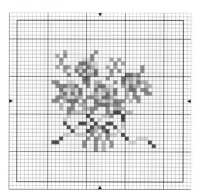

Fig 5.39 **Chart for Rose Posy chair seat.**

Rose Posy Chair Back and Seat

		Skeins	DMC	Anchor	Madeira
	Dark blue	1	798	137	0911
	Light blue	1	827	9159	1014
	Dark pink	1	602	63	0702
	Mid pink	1	899	66	0609
	Light pink	1	776	24	0607
	Mauve	1	554	96	0711
	Dark green	1	470	266	1410
	Light green	1	472	264	1414
Alternative backgrounds					
	Cream (on chart)	1	Ecru	926	Ecru
	Light green	1	504	1042	1701

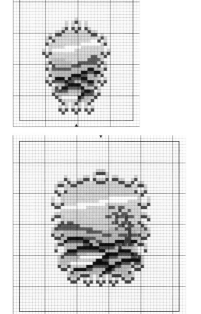

Fig 5.40 **Landscape design (chair seat and back).**

Fig 5.41 **Charts for Landscape chair seat and back.**

Footstools

All four designs can be worked within any shape or size, and can be used for round, square or rectangular footstools, cushions, chair covers or screens. Simply mark the desired shape onto the fabric and work the patterns within the shape.

Landscape design

This landscape design can be used for any time during the whole Georgian period. The example pictured here (*see* Fig 5.40 and the chart in Fig 5.41) has been worked on a natural-coloured linen. As with the Rose Posy set, a white linen background could be coloured as an alternative.

Landscape Chair Back and Seat

		Skeins	DMC	Anchor	Madeira
	Gold	I	725	305	0106
	Brown	I	433	371	2008
	Light green	I	472	264	1414
	Mid green	I	320	216	1311
	Dark green	I	986	246	1313
	Blue	I	827	9159	1014
	White	I	Blanc	White	White

Alternative backgrounds

	Cream (on chart)	I	677	886	2207
	Dark red	I	816	1005	0512
	Blue	I	798	137	0911
	Green	I	986	246	1313

Fig 5.42 **Completed trompe l'oeil footstools.**

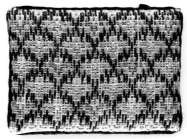

Fig 5.43 **Completed Florentine footstools.**

Trompe l'oeil Footstools

During the eighteenth century the Georgians were particularly fascinated by illusions. One very popular form of illusion was trompe l'oeil – 'deception of the eye' – a style of painting on a surface to create the impression of a three-dimensional object. Many large country houses and stately homes have excellent examples. In particular, at Chatsworth House in Derbyshire, a perfectly flat communicating door has been painted to look like a panelled door with a violin hanging on it.

The ladies of the time liked to imitate this style in the designs of their embroidery. The first two projects in this chapter are based on two late-1750s stool tops at Arbury Hall, Nuneaton, Warwickshire. The stool tops were worked by Sophia Conyers, the first wife of Sir Richard Newdigate, who transformed the original Elizabethan house into eighteenth-century 'Gothick'. Legend has it that when Sophia asked her husband what design to use on a set of stools, he said she should work 'what lay upon them'. Thus one shows a fan and handkerchief, the second two books.

The two trompe l'oeil designs shown here have been worked on linen that has been coloured. Complete instructions for this process are given in Chapter 15.

Alternatively, the background can be worked in tent stitch in one of the colours suggested, or in one of your own choice.

Trompe l'oeil Footstools

Materials

For each footstool

Evenweave linen (35 count): 100mm (4in) square

Stranded cotton as listed in colour key

Tapestry needle: No. 24 or 26

Card mount OR

Small embroidery frame

Wood glue

Wood stain

Satin varnish

Thin card

For each round footstool

Button mould OR

Button with shank filed off

Stripwood, obeche or jelutong: 2–3mm (⅛in) thick

Wooden beads x 3

For each rectangular or square footstool

Felt

Stripwood, obeche or jelutong: 3–5mm (⅛–³⁄₁₆in) thick, 40mm (1½in) wide

Wooden beads x 3 or 4 OR

Small cabriole legs x 4

Approximate sizes

Rectangular footstool

42 x 30mm (1⅝ x 1³⁄₁₆in)

Square footstool

As required

Round footstool

As required

Working method

1 If you wish to colour the fabric, do this first (*see* Chapter 15).

2 Mount the fabric in a card frame (*see* Chapter 13).

3 Mark the outline of the footstool on the fabric with small tacking stitches.

4 Mark the horizontal and vertical centres, again with small tacking stitches.

5 Select the required chart from Fig 5.44 or 5.45.

6 Begin to work the design from the centre, using one strand of stranded cotton and tent stitch throughout.

7 If the fabric was not coloured, fill in the background in tent stitch in your desired colour to the outline.

8 Make up the footstool as shown later in this chapter.

Fan and 'Kerchief Footstool

		Skeins	DMC	Anchor	Madeira
	Light pink	1	224	893	0813
	Dark pink	1	223	895	0812
	White	1	Blanc	White	White
	Light grey	1	648	900	1902
	Dark grey	1	451	233	1808
	Cream	1	677	886	2207
	Gold	1	437	362	2012
	Blue grey	1	926	850	1707

Alternative backgrounds

	Light green (on chart)	1	504	1042	1701
	Dark red	1	816	1005	1512
	Blue	1	798	137	0911

Books Footstool

		Skeins	DMC	Anchor	Madeira
	Gold	1	437	362	2012
	Cream	1	677	886	2207
	Red	1	350	11	0213
	Light grey	1	648	900	1902
	Blue grey	1	926	850	1707
	White	1	Blanc	White	White

Alternative backgrounds

	Light green (on chart)	1	504	1042	1701
	Dark red	1	816	1005	1512
	Blue	1	798	137	0911

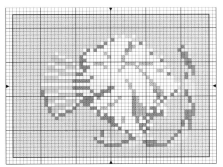

Fig 5.44 **Chart for Fan and 'Kerchief footstool.**

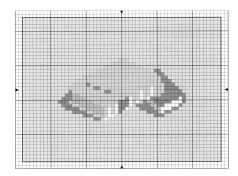

Fig 5.45 **Chart for Books footstool.**

Florentine Footstools

These two designs are all-over Florentine patterns, a technique popular throughout the Georgian era.

Working method

1 Mount and mark the fabric as above.

2 Select the required chart.

3 Begin in the centre, using one strand of cotton and straight vertical stitches as shown on the charts.

Square Florentine Footstool

		Skeins	DMC	Anchor	Madeira
	Blue	I	926	850	1707
	Dark pink	I	602	63	0702
	Light pink	I	224	893	0813
	Ecru	I	Ecru	926	Ecru
	Dark green	I	320	216	1311
	Light green	I	504	1042	1701

Rectangular Florentine Footstool

		Skeins	DMC	Anchor	Madeira
	Dark green	I	986	246	1313
	Light green	I	504	1042	1701
	Pink	I	899	66	0609
	Blue	I	827	9159	1014
	Gold	I	3046	887	2206
	Cream	I	Ecru	926	Ecru

Florentine Footstools

Materials

For each footstool

Evenweave linen (40 count): 100mm (4in) square

Stranded cotton as indicated in colour key

Tapestry needle: No. 26

Card mount OR

Small embroidery frame

Wood glue

Wood stain

Satin varnish

Thin card

For each round footstool

Button mould OR

Button with shank filed off

Stripwood, obeche or jelutong: 2–3mm (⅛in) thick

Wooden beads x 3

For each rectangular or square footstool

Felt

Stripwood, obeche or jelutong: 3-5mm (⅛–³⁄₁₆in) thick, 40mm (1½in) wide

Wooden beads x 3 or 4 OR

Small cabriole legs x 4

Approximate sizes

Rectangular footstool

42 x 30mm (1⅝ x 1³⁄₁₆in)

Square footstool

30mm (1³⁄₁₆in) square

Round footstool

As required

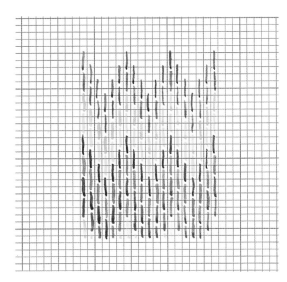

Fig 5.46 **Chart for square Florentine footstool.**

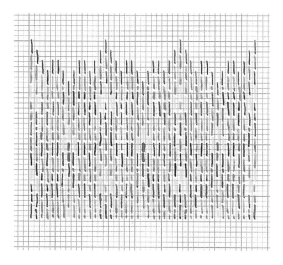

Fig 5.47 **Chart for rectangular Florentine footstool.**

4 Continue the pattern until the required shape and size is filled. Make up the footstool as follows.

Making up the footstools

Rectangular and square footstools

Cut a piece of thin card to the required size, which is slightly smaller than your embroidery (A in Fig 5.48).

Cut a piece of felt slightly smaller than the card. If the felt is very thin, use two layers. Secure the felt to the upper side of the card with a small spot of glue (B in Fig 5.48).

Lay the embroidery over the felt and card and check that the embroidery reaches over the edges of the card. If it does not, cut a little from around the edges of the card. When you are satisfied, secure two opposite turnings to the underside of the card, using glue very sparingly (C in Fig 5.48). Leave to dry.

Trim a little excess fabric from the corners and secure the two remaining turnings in the same way. Leave to dry.

Now that the card is covered, measure the size and cut the wooden base from stripwood. The wooden base should extend about 1mm around the edges.

Attach either beads or cabriole legs to the underside of the wooden base. Stain and varnish this as desired (D in Fig 5.48).

Finally, glue the embroidered stool top into position (E in Fig 5.48).

Fig 5.48 **Making up a square or rectangular footstool.**

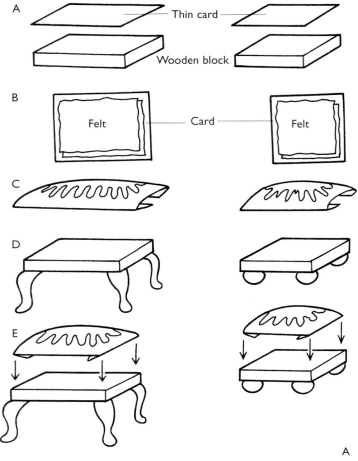

Cut a template from the thin card the same size as the button mould (A in Fig 5.49). Lay the template on the embroidered piece, making sure that the design is central. Trim the fabric around the edge to about 10mm (⅜in).

Fasten on securely and work a gathering thread around the turning, about 5mm (³⁄₁₆in) from the edge (C in Fig 5.49).

Place the embroidered circle into position over the button mould and draw up the gathering thread. When the embroidery is in the correct position, fasten off the gathering thread (D in Fig 5.49).

Finally, using glue very sparingly, attach the covered button mould to the prepared wooden base (E in Fig 5.49).

Round footstools

If you are using a commercial kit, follow the manufacturer's instructions.

Using the button mould as a guide, draw around it onto the stripwood. The circle on the wood will be a little larger than the button mould.

Cut out the circle of wood. The easiest way is to cut a square, then remove the corners with a diagonal cut. Gently rub down to a circle with sandpaper. Glue three beads to the underside of the wooden base and stain, then varnish this as desired (*see* E in Fig 5.49). Leave to dry.

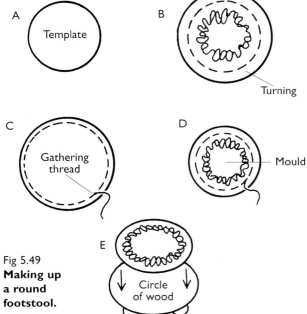

Fig 5.49
Making up a round footstool.

6 Screens

Three types of screens were used during the Georgian period. Pole screens were small decorative panels, mounted on a floor-standing pole which allowed the height of the screen to be adjusted. The screens were decorated with embroidered, tapestry woven or painted panels. These were either mounted rigidly in a frame or, if embroidered or woven, could hang like a small banner. The pole screens were placed between a lady's face and the direct heat of a fire to protect her complexion.

Fire screens were decorative panels on legs or feet which would stand in the fireplace when it was not in use.

Taller folding screens of two, three or four panels were used to give protection from draughts or for privacy.

The designs given here for the pole and fire screens are also suitable for use as pictures.

The charts for the canvaswork cushions in Chapter 5 (*see* pages 51–3) can be adapted for use as pole screens by substituting a 35 count evenweave linen for the canvas, and working with a single thread of stranded cotton.

Three-fold screens

Pastoral Landscape Screen

The design for this three-fold screen (Fig 6.1) is based on one worked by Lady Julia Calverley dated 1727. The original can be seen at the National Trust's Wallington Hall in Northumberland.

This screen reflects a style of canvaswork which was popular during the seventeenth century, continuing into the eighteenth, especially in rural areas where fashions were slower to change. The

Fig 6.1 **Pastoral Landscape three-fold screen.**

main theme is rural life, with the first panel (*see* Fig 6.2) showing an attempt to catch a swarm of bees. It also contains a 'folly' within the grounds of the house, a popular feature with the landscape designers of the time.

The second panel depicts the lady of the house selecting flowers, which are placed in a basket by a servant. The final panel shows a worker by a pool, making baskets. The pool is fed by a waterfall, another favourite feature of the eighteenth-century designers.

Fig 6.2 **Pastoral Landscape design.**

Pastoral Landscape Screen

Materials

Evenweave linen (35 count):
  220 x 200mm (8½ x 8in)
Stranded cotton as listed in colour key
Rectangular embroidery frame
Tapestry needle: No. 24 or 26
Tacking cotton
Razor saw or craft knife
Leather, suede or Vilene interlining:
  220 x 200mm (8½ x 8in)

Stripwood:
  2 x 45 x 450mm (⅟₁₆ x 1¾ x 18in)
  2 x 6 x 1140mm (⅟₁₆ x ¼ x 45in)
  2 x 12 x 140mm (⅟₁₆ x ½ x 6in)
Stain and varnish as desired
PVA wood glue

Size

Each panel
126 x 31mm (5 x 1¼in)
Completed screen
146 x 135mm (5¾ x 5¼in)

Pastoral Landscape Screen

		Skeins	DMC	Anchor	Madeira
	Dark green	I	319	683	I3I3
	Mid green	I	320	216	I3II
	Light green	I	368	214	I3I0
	Very pale green	I	369	I043	I309
	Dark leaf green	I	470	266	I4I0
	Light leaf green	I	472	264	I4I4
	Dark brown	I	839	I050	I9I3
	Light brown	I	84I	378	I9II
	Honey	I	3045	888	2I03
	Dark cream	I	3046	887	2206
	Light cream	I	739	I009	20I4
	Bright yellow	I	444	297	0I05
	Red	I	8I6	I005	05I2
	Dark peach	I	352	9	0303
	Flesh	I	95I	880	2308
	Mid blue	I	798	I37	09II
	Light blue	I	827	9I59	I0I4
	Mid grey	I	926	850	I707
	Light grey	I	928	274	I708
	White	I	Blanc	White	White

Preparation

To prepare the fabric, mark the outer edges of each panel with tacking stitches. Leave about 25mm (1in) of fabric in between the three panels to allow for making up. Mount the fabric into the embroidery frame.

Working method

Using the chart from Fig 6.3, begin the design from the bottom of each panel. Each square on the chart represents one stitch. Use one strand of stranded cotton in tent stitch throughout.

When the embroidery is complete, remove it from the frame, and mount and finish as shown later in this chapter. If the embroidery has distorted, block it into shape as shown in Chapter 16 (*see* page 173) before making up.

Fig 6.3 **Chart for Pastoral Landscape screen.**

Fig 6.4 **Crewel Work three-fold screen.**

Crewel Work Screen

The design for this screen (see Figs 6.4 and 6.5) shows the light, airy crewel work of the early eighteenth century. The use of an exotic bird reflects the fashion for Chinoiserie that began in the previous century and continued into the

nineteenth. The term 'Chinoiserie' was given to a style which Europeans thought was Chinese but which, in reality, bore no resemblance to actual Chinese art. This project is suited to the first half of the eighteenth century.

Fig 6.5 **Crewel Work design.**

Crewel Work Screen

Materials

Lightweight silk or cotton fabric:
   220 x 200mm (8½ x 8in)
Stranded cotton as listed in colour key
Embroidery or quilting needle: No. 10
Tacking cotton
PVA wood glue
Razor saw or craft knife
Leather, suede or Vilene interlining:
   220 x 200mm (8½ x 8in)

Stripwood:
   2 x 45 x 450mm (1/16 x 1¾ x 18in)
   2 x 6 x 1140mm (1/16 x ¼ x 45in)
   2 x 12 x 140mm (1/16 x ½ x 6in)
Stain and varnish as desired

Size
Each panel
126 x 31mm (5 x 1¼in)
Completed screen
146 x 135mm (5¾ x 5¼in)

Fig 6.6 **Pattern for Crewel Work screen.**

Preparation

Prepare the fabric by tacking an outline for each panel, leaving about 25mm (1in) between each one.

Transfer the design from Fig 6.6 into position within each outline. Use the tracing method if the fabric is fine enough to see through, or dressmakers' carbon, or iron off a photocopy. Remember the photocopy method will reverse the design. Details of all these methods can be found in Chapter 14. Mount the fabric into an embroidery frame.

Working method

On the example shown, each panel has a different coloured bird. Any two shades of a colour can be substituted as desired. Work the design using the stitch and colour diagram (*see* Fig 6.7) as a guide. Use one strand of stranded cotton and backstitch throughout.

Crewel Work Screen

		Skeins	DMC	Anchor	Madeira
	Dark green	I	937	268	1504
	Mid green	I	470	266	1410
	Light green	I	472	264	1414
	Dark peach	I	352	9	0303
	Light peach	I	353	868	0304
Alternative bird colours:					
	Bright blue	I	996	433	1103
	Turquoise	I	958	187	1114
	Orange	I	740	316	0202
	Gold	I	742	303	0107

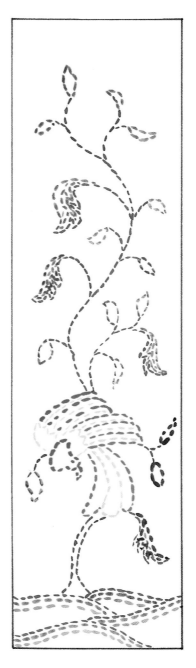

Fig 6.7 **Stitch pattern for Crewel Work screen.**

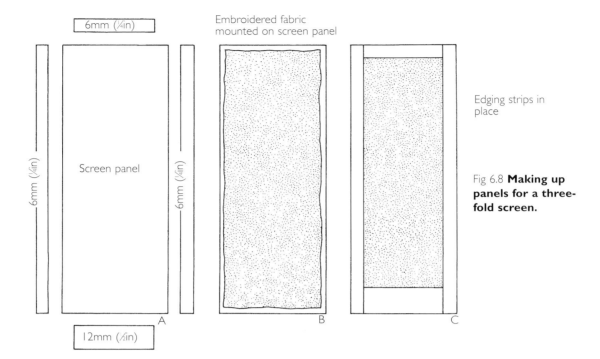

6mm (¼in)

Embroidered fabric
mounted on screen panel

Edging strips in
place

Fig 6.8 **Making up
panels for a three-
fold screen.**

6mm (¼in)

Screen panel

6mm (¼in)

A

B

C

12mm (½in)

Initially, it is possible to start with a small knot in the thread. Once an area of stitching has been worked, new threads can be started and finished off by working them into the back of the stitching.

When the embroidery is complete, remove it from the frame and make up the screen as indicated later in this chapter.

Making up a three-fold screen

1 Stain all stripwood as desired.

2 Using the widest stripwood, cut three pieces 146mm (5¾in) long. These are the three screen panels (*see* Fig 6.8A).

3 Cover the front of each screen panel with a thin coat of PVA glue. Drag the edge of a piece of card across the surface to remove any excess glue. Allow the glue to dry completely.

4 Place the embroidered panels over the dried glue. Leave 6mm (¼in) at top and 12mm (½in) at lower edge to allow for the edging strips.

5 With a warm iron (set to the correct temperature for the fabric used) seal the edges of the fabric to the wood. The heat on the dry PVA will dry mount the edges of the fabric (*see* Fig 6.8B).

6 Cut 6 lengths of the 6mm (¼in) wide stripwood to the same length as the screen panels (*see* Fig 6.8A).

7 Using the wood glue sparingly, glue one strip to each long side of the screen panels.

8 Cut a piece of 6mm (¼in) stripwood to fit between the two side strips, across the top edge of each screen panel.

9 Cut a piece of 12mm (½in) stripwood to fit between the two side strips, across the lower edge of each screen panel.

10 Glue into position as above (*see* Fig 6.8C).

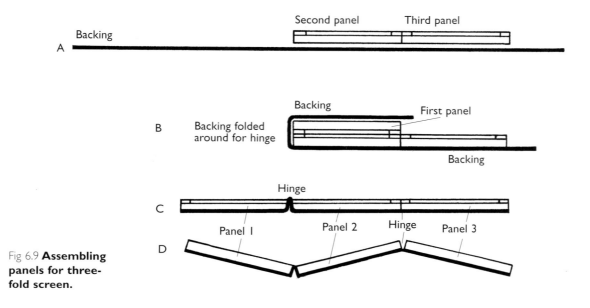

Fig 6.9 **Assembling panels for three-fold screen.**

Assembling and hinging the panels

1 Place the leather, suede or Vilene backing face down onto the work surface. (The Vilene can be coloured if desired.) Do not cut to shape: the backing should be larger than the completed screen.

2 Spread PVA glue sparingly on the back of the second and third screen panels and place them side by side onto the backing, close together (*see* Fig 6.9A). Allow the glue to dry completely.

3 Place the first screen panel face down on top of the second panel.

4 Spread glue over the backing beside the two panels, and fold the backing up and over the back of the first panel. Make sure the edges are secured to the backing, as this forms a hinge (*see* Fig 6.9B and C). Allow to dry completely.

5 Finally, with a sharp craft knife, cut the surplus backing away from the edges of the screen. The panels will now hinge into a zigzag and stand upright (*see* Fig 6.9D).

Fig 6.10 **Chinese Vase fire screen.**

Fire screens

Chinese Vase Screen

This design has been adapted from an embroidered panel dated to the second quarter of the eighteenth century (*see* Fig 6.11). The original, in the Victoria and Albert Museum, is worked in surface embroidery in silks on a satin ground. It shows a Chinoiserie vase with naturalistic flowers.

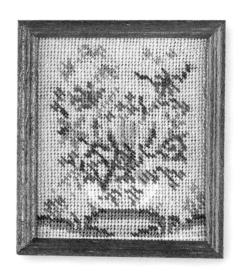

Fig 6.11 **Chinese Vase design.**

Chinese Vase Screen

Materials

Evenweave linen (35 count): 100mm (4in) square

Stranded cotton as listed in colour key

Tapestry needle: No. 24 or 26

Tacking cotton

Mounting card: 100mm (4in) square

Miniature picture frame moulding, without rebate: 300mm (12in)

Stripwood: 5 x 5 x 40mm (³⁄₁₆ x ³⁄₁₆ x 1½in)

PVA wood glue

Stain and varnish as desired

Size

45 x 36mm (1¾ x 1⁷⁄₁₆in)

Chinese Vase Fire Screen

		Skeins	DMC	Anchor	Madeira
	Red	1	816	1005	0512
	Peach	1	352	9	0303
	Light peach	1	950	376	2309
	Dull pink	1	316	1017	0809
	Orange	1	741	314	0201
	Light terracotta	1	407	914	2312
	Honey	1	3045	888	2103
	Dark cream	1	3046	887	2206
	Mid blue	1	798	137	0911
	Light blue	1	827	9159	1014
	Dark green	1	319	683	1313
	Mid green	1	320	216	1311
	Light green	1	369	1043	1309
	White	1	Blanc	White	White
	Cream	1	739	1009	2014

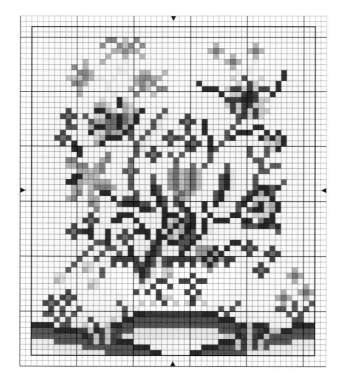

Fig 6.12 **Chart for Chinese Vase fire screen.**

Fig 6.13 **Chinoiserie fire screen.**

Chinoiserie Screen

This screen (*see* Fig 6.14) is based on a panel thought to have been worked by a Scottish embroiderer. The original, c.1750, can be seen in the Palace of Holyrood House in Edinburgh. The design shows exotic birds in a flowering tree, above a carp leaping from a pond. The whole is set within a cartouche (an ornate framework) surrounded by flowers.

Fig 6.14 **Chinoiserie design.**

Chinoiserie Screen

Materials

Evenweave linen (35 count): 100mm (4in) square

Stranded cotton as listed in colour key

Tapestry needle: No. 24 or 26

Tacking cotton

Mounting card: 100mm (4in) square

Miniature picture frame moulding without a rebate: 300mm (12in)

Stripwood: 5 x 5 x 40mm (³⁄₁₆ x ³⁄₁₆ x 1½in)

PVA wood glue

Stain and varnish as desired

Size

45 x 36mm (1¾ x 1⁷⁄₁₆in)

Chinoiserie Fire Screen

		Skeins	DMC	Anchor	Madeira
	Honey	1	3045	888	2103
	Dark cream	1	3046	887	2206
	Orange	1	741	314	0201
	Dark orange	1	921	1003	0311
	Light blue	1	827	9159	1014
	Bright blue	1	996	433	1103
	Turquoise	1	958	187	1114
	Dark green	1	470	266	1410
	Light green	1	472	264	1414
	Dark brown	1	839	1050	1913
	Light brown	1	841	378	1911
	Dark peach	1	352	9	0303
	Light peach	1	951	880	2308
	Dark grey blue	1	926	850	1707
	Light grey blue	1	928	274	1708
	Dark pink	1	335	38	0610
	White	1	Blanc	White	White

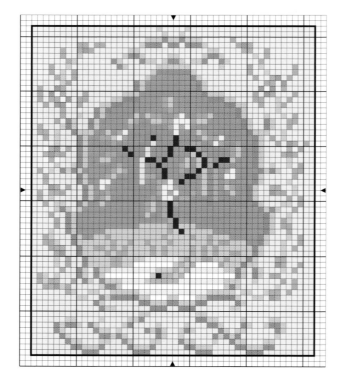

Fig 6.15 **Chart for Chinoiserie fire screen.**

Working method for fire screens

1 Mount the fabric in a card frame (*see* Chapter 13).

2 Mark the outlines and the vertical and horizontal centres with tacking stitches.

3 Select the required chart (*see* Fig 6.12 or 6.15). Each square represents one stitch.

4 Begin to stitch from the centre, using one strand of stranded cotton in tent stitch throughout. Work the design first and then fill in the background.

5 When the embroidery is complete, remove it from the card frame. Block the piece if it has distorted (*see* Chapter 16).

6 Make up the fire screen as shown later in this chapter.

Making up a fire screen

If you are using a commercially produced fire screen kit, follow the manufacturer's instructions. Alternatively, if you are making your own, follow the instructions below.

1 Mount the embroidery onto the square of card, and cut and mitre the miniature moulding as directed in Fig 8.24 (*see* page 107). The inside edge measurements should equal the finished size of the embroidery.

2 Glue the pieces of the frame together at the corners using glue sparingly.

3 When dry, place the frame into position over the embroidery and glue into place. Allow to dry completely (*see* Fig 6.16).

Fig 6.16 **Making up a fire screen.**

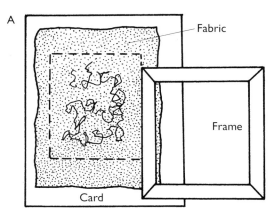

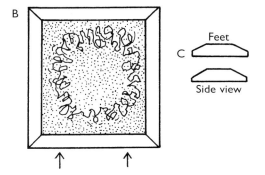

4 Carefully cut away the excess card and fabric from around the edges of the frame with a sharp craft knife.

5 To make the feet, cut the 5mm (³⁄₁₆in) stripwood into two lengths each 15mm (½in) long. Sand the two top corners slightly to round them, leaving the bottom two corners square. Glue the two feet to the lower edge of the fire screen frame so that the feet extend equally to the front and back. (*See* the completed firescreen in Fig 6.10.)

Fig 6.17 **Pole screens.**

Pole Screens

The two pole screens shown in Fig 6.17 use charts given for other projects. The design for the round screen uses the centre section of Fig 6.15, the chart for the Chinoiserie fire screen. The pole screen has been worked on 40 count evenweave linen. The linen has been coloured prior to use so that the background does not have to be worked. (For methods of colouring fabric please refer to Chapter 15.)

The round screen has been mounted within a commercial screen kit, but it could equally well be made up as shown later in this chapter.

The Rose Posy pole screen is the same as the chair back and seat design from Chapter 5 (*see* page 68) and uses Fig 5.39. The example shown here has been worked on a 35 count cream-coloured evenweave linen. The linen could be coloured as suggested above if desired.

The working method for embroidering a pole screen is exactly the same as for a fire screen. (Refer to the instructions given on page 87.)

Pole Screens

Materials

Evenweave linen (35 or 40 count): 100mm (4in) square

Stranded cotton as listed in colour key

Tapestry needle: No. 24 or 26

Tacking cotton

Card and miniature picture moulding as for the fire screens

Turned baluster x 1 OR

Dowelling, 3mm (⅛in): 100mm (4in)

Stripwood, 3mm (⅛in): 30mm (1¼in) square

Wooden beads, approximately 5mm (³⁄₁₆in) diameter x 3

PVA wood glue

Stain and varnish as desired

Size

As required

Making up a pole screen

If you are using a commercially made kit, follow the manufacturer's instructions. To make your own, follow the instructions below.

1 Mount and frame the embroidery as described for the fire screens.

2 Cut the base from the stripwood, using the pattern given in Fig 6.18C, and drill a hole in the centre to the correct size for the baluster or dowelling.

3 Cut the dowelling to length (*see* Fig 6.18A).

4 Glue the three beads onto the underside of the base and glue the dowelling or baluster into the hole in the base.

5 Stain and varnish as required.

6 Glue the framed pole screen into position on the dowelling or baluster (*see* finished screens in Fig 6.17).

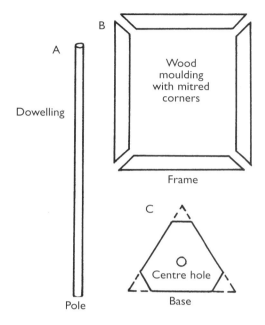

Fig 6.18 **Making up a pole screen.**

7 Table coverings

During the Georgian period people took great pride in showing off their furniture to the best advantage. This meant that a cloth was very rarely used on a dining table, but a wealthy household might boast of having a French chef in the kitchen, who would insist on having a white linen cloth on his kitchen table.

Instructions for a basic tablecloth are given for those who wish to cover their miniature tables.

Drafting a pattern

Miniature tables will vary in size and each will need an individual pattern (*see* Fig 7.1).

1 Measure the width and length of the table top and draw the outline on a sheet of paper. Alternatively, lay the table top on the paper and draw around the edge.

2 Extend the lines outwards to allow for the drop. This will probably be 35mm (1⅜in) for most tables.

3 Add a further 6mm (¼in) as a hem allowance.

Linen cloth

Working method

1 Cut the fabric to the size of your paper pattern.

2 Turn a narrow hem around the edges and stitch to secure.

3 A narrow lace edging can be added if required. This can be stitched in place, or attached with PVA fabric glue, used sparingly.

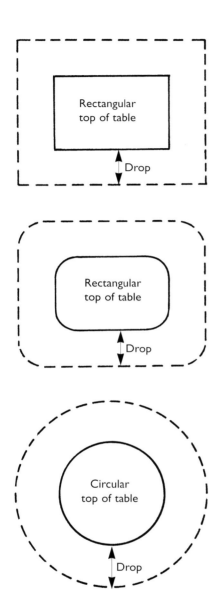

Fig 7.1 **Making a pattern for a table cover.**

Linen Cloth

Materials

Lightweight cotton lawn or handkerchief fabric:
    to size of pattern
Sewing thread
Embroidery needle: No. 10
Narrow lace (optional)
PVA fabric glue

Size

As required

Fitting the cloth

1 Completely cover the table with plastic clingfilm, ensuring that the film is smooth and tight across the top of the table.

2 Make a solution of diluted PVA glue and water, one part glue to three parts water.

3 Paint the solution onto the underside of the cloth and place the cloth over the table top, smoothing the surface to remove any air bubbles.

4 Arrange and drape the cloth neatly and evenly around the sides.

5 Leave to dry completely.

6 When dry, the cloth will be stiff and shaped to the table. Gently ease the cloth from the table, remove the clingfilm, and replace the cloth on the table.

This method can be followed using spray starch. However, be warned: the starch can encourage tiny bugs into your dolls' house.

8 Pictures and samplers

During the eighteenth century embroidered pictures were very popular, especially those done in canvaswork. It was possible, during this time, to purchase canvas and fabric with the designs already prepared, or to have a design of your own choice prepared professionally. The pictures would usually be based on popular classical paintings or engravings, often pastoral scenes.

Botanical painting reached its height during the eighteenth century. The beautiful, naturalistic flowers provided an ideal subject for embroidery design. There was also a strong influence of Chinoiserie. Flowers were often shown placed in vases or bowls in the style of Chinese porcelain, frequently standing on a black-and-white 'tiled' table. The manner of painting flowers followed by the Dutch painters was reflected in the large, open blooms. Many examples of a strange mix of these styles can be found.

The pictures worked on canvas would have been drawn in outline on the canvas and the embroiderer would fill in the colours in fine worsted wools or with silk.

Those worked on a silk ground would have the details drawn in a fine outline with the sky and any faces and hands painted in watercolour. In addition to pastoral scenes, there were sometimes mourning pictures showing a young girl in classical dress next to a tomb. The embroiderer would use long and short, split and satin stitches to work the background details and dress. Sometimes the foliage on the trees was stitched with a fine silk chenille thread, giving a lovely silky texture.

In addition to the two projects given here, any of the cushion, fire or pole screen charts can be used as pictures as shown in Fig 8.1.

Fig 8.1 **Pictures using Chinoiserie fire screen (see Fig 6.15) and Rose Posy chair cover (see Fig 5.39) designs.**

The four floral canvaswork cushions (*see* pages 51–3) are worked on 22 count canvas. If a smaller picture is required, either substitute a 27 count linen using two strands of stranded cotton, or a 35 count linen using one strand of stranded cotton.

The sampler of the eighteenth century was very much a schoolroom exercise to show a young lady's competence with a needle. No longer the stitch and pattern record of earlier centuries, it was designed to be displayed.

The projects in this chapter are all based on the collection of samplers in the Fitzwilliam Museum in Cambridge. All the originals were worked on a woollen canvas with silk embroidery threads.

Canvaswork pictures

Pot of Flowers

The design shown in Fig 8.2 has been based on a canvaswork panel from the second quarter of the eighteenth century, which can be found in the Victoria and Albert Museum, London. It is a good example of Dutch-style flowers in a Chinese pot on a black-and-white tiled table.

Fig 8.2 **Pot of Flowers picture.**

Pot of Flowers

Materials

Evenweave linen (40 count): 100mm (4in) square

Stranded cotton as listed in colour key

Tapestry needle: No. 26

Card frame

Miniature picture frame moulding: 300mm (12in)

Mounting card: 100mm (4in) square

PVA glue

Size

60 stitches square

38mm (1½in) square

Pot of Flowers Picture

		Skeins	DMC	Anchor	Madeira
	Light green	1	3053	260	1603
	Dark green	1	3051	268	1508
	Light pink	1	3326	36	0606
	Dark pink	1	335	38	0610
	Light blue	1	827	9159	1014
	Dark blue	1	798	137	0911
	Yellow	1	3046	887	2206
	Gold	1	3045	888	2103
	Red	1	321	47	0510
	Black	1	310	Black	Black
	White	1	Blanc	White	White

Fig 8.3 **Chart for Pot of Flowers picture.**

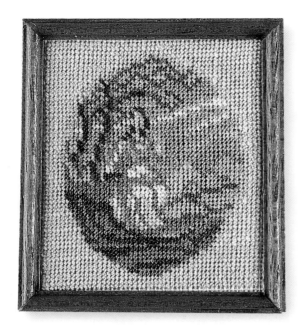

Fig 8.4 **Lady in a Landscape picture.**

Lady in a Landscape

The design in Fig 8.4 is typical of many such pictures. It is based on a silk picture, c.1790, with watercolour details on the background.

Preparation

Mount the linen in the card frame as described in Chapter 13. Mark the vertical and horizontal centres with small tacking stitches.

Working method

Select the required chart from Figs 8.3 and 8.5, or others as suggested above. Using one strand of stranded cotton and tent stitch throughout, begin near the centre. Remove the tacking stitches as soon as a small area of stitching has been worked. When the design has been completed, fill in the background colour. Remove from the card frame, then mount and frame as described on pages 107 and 108.

Lady in a Landscape

Materials

Evenweave linen (40 count): 100mm (4in) square
Stranded cotton as listed in colour key
Tapestry needle: No. 26
Card frame
Miniature picture frame moulding: 300mm (12in) length
Mounting card: 100mm (4in) square
PVA glue

Size

60 x 50 stitches
38 x 32mm (1½ x 1¼in)

Lady in a Landscape Picture

		Skeins	DMC	Anchor	Madeira
	Cream	I	739	1009	2014
	Grey	I	928	274	1708
	Light mauve	I	3042	870	0807
	Light blue green	I	504	1042	1701
	Dark blue green	I	502	876	1703
	Light green	I	3053	260	1603
	Dark green	I	3051	268	1508
	Brown	I	839	1050	1913
	Gold	I	3045	888	2103
	Pale blue grey	I	3072	234	1805
	Blue	I	827	9159	1014
	White	I	Blanc	White	White
	Dark peach	I	352	9	0303
	Light peach	I	353	868	0304

Fig 8.5 **Chart for Lady in a Landscape picture.**

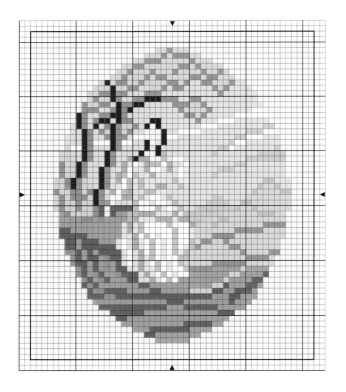

Samplers

The projects below have been worked on a 40 count evenweave linen. If a 32 or 35 count linen is substituted, the sampler will be a little larger than the size quoted below.

Preparation

Mount the fabric in the card frame (*see* Chapter 13). Mark the outer edges and the vertical and horizontal centres with small tacking stitches.

Working method

Refer to your chosen chart. A solid square on the chart represents a tent stitch and a vertical, horizontal or diagonal line represents a straight stitch with the corresponding orientation.

For all designs, begin by working the border, as this will make it easier to position the motifs. When you have completed the embroidery, remove the fabric from the card frame, then mount and frame the sampler using the method given on pages 107 and 108.

Samplers

Materials

For each sampler

Evenweave linen (40–35 count): 100mm (4in) square

Stranded cotton as listed in colour key

Tapestry needle: No. 26

Card frame

Sizes

Design 1
66 x 45 stitches
41 x 28mm (1⅝ x 1⅛in)

Design 2
66 x 45 stitches
41 x 28mm (1⅝ x 1⅛in)

Design 3
56 x 37 stitches
35 x 23mm (1⅜ x ⅞in)

Design 4
57 stitches square
35mm (1⅜in) square

Design 5
54 x 35 stitches
35 x 22mm (1⅜ x ⅞in)

Design 6
57 stitches square
35mm (1⅜in) square

Design 7
56 x 37 stitches
35 x 23mm (1⅜ x ⅞in)

Design 8
70 x 50 stitches
45 x 33mm (1¾ x 1 5/16in)

Design 9
69 x 49 stitches
44 x 32mm (1¾ x 1¼in)

Design 1

Follow Fig 8.7. The original is signed and dated 'Hetty Grigg, 1761', and reads: 'I'll be sincere and upright and true at home at schoo…l and elsewhere'. The sampler (Fig 8.6) features a house, verse and black-and-white paved area.

Fig 8.6 **Sampler, Design 1.**

Fig 8.7 **Chart for sampler, Design 1.**

Sampler – Design 1

		Skeins	DMC	Anchor	Madeira
	Dark green	1	319	683	1313
	Light green	1	369	1043	1309
	Red	1	321	47	0510
	Blue	1	799	145	0910
	Yellow	1	676	891	2208
	Black	1	310	Black	Black
	White	1	Blanc	White	White

Design 2

Follow Fig 8.9. Dated 1762, the original is signed 'Ann Hair aged 14'. This sampler reflects the samplers of the seventeenth century, with bands of patterns, one of which shows stag hunting (Fig 8.8).

Fig 8.8 **Sampler, Design 2.**

Fig 8.9 **Chart for sampler, Design 2.**

Sampler – Design 2

		Skeins	DMC	Anchor	Madeira
	Dark green	1	319	683	1313
	Light green	1	369	1043	1309
	Yellow	1	676	891	2208
	Blue	1	799	145	0910
	Peach	1	352	9	0303
	Dark peach	1	407	914	2312
	Dark brown	1	839	1050	1913
	Light brown	1	841	378	1911

99

Design 3

Follow Fig 8.11. This sampler is based on an original signed by Ann Smith and dated 1767. Bands of pattern show flowers, trees and Adam and Eve. Two little lions rampant fill the lower corners (Fig 8.10).

Fig 8.10 **Sampler, Design 3.**

Fig 8.11 **Chart for sampler, Design 3.**

Sampler – Design 3

		Skeins	DMC	Anchor	Madeira
	Dark green	1	319	683	1313
	Light green	1	369	1043	1309
	Dark brown	1	839	1050	1913
	Light brown	1	841	378	1911
	Mid blue	1	799	145	0910
	Light blue	1	827	9159	1014
	Red	1	816	1005	0512
	Light yellow	1	3046	887	2206
	Mid yellows	1	3045	888	2103
	Dark pink	1	316	1017	0809

Design 4

Follow Fig 8.13. The original sampler contains spot motifs, some of which are worked in surface stitchery. It is dated 1773 and signed 'Anna Maria Dobson, 11 years old'. The verse on the original reads: 'Wisdom the greatest blessing from above sent by God in his great love' (Fig 8.12).

Fig 8.12 **Sampler, Design 4.**

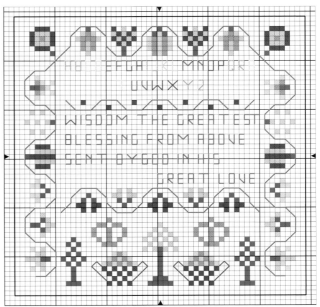

Fig 8.13 **Chart for sampler, Design 4.**

Sampler – Design 4

		Skeins	DMC	Anchor	Madeira
	Red	1	816	1005	0512
	Pink	1	316	1017	0809
	Blue	1	799	145	0910
	Yellow	1	3046	887	2206
	Gold	1	3045	888	2103
	Green	1	319	683	1313

Design 5

Follow Fig 8.15. The original sampler on which this project is based was worked in surface stitchery with a counted thread border. Signed 'Mary Brooks', it is dated 1792. The verse is: 'How doth the little busy bee improve each shining hour' (Fig 8.14).

Fig 8.14 **Sampler, Design 5.**　　　Fig 8.15 **Chart for sampler, Design 5.**

Sampler – Design 5

		Skeins	DMC	Anchor	Madeira
	Pink	I	776	24	0607
	Peach	I	352	9	0303
	Dark green	I	319	683	1313
	Yellow	I	3046	887	2206
	Olive green	I	730	924	1614
	Light olive green	I	470	266	1410
	Blue	I	799	145	0910

Design 6

Follow Fig 8.17. The original is signed 'Sarah Stuart, 1798', with spot motifs in surface stitchery and counted thread. The project (Fig 8.16) features a house and various plant forms in pots.

Fig 8.16 **Sampler, Design 6.**

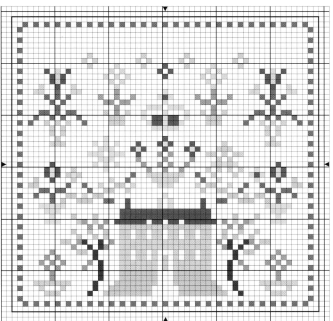

Fig 8.17 **Chart for sampler, Design 6.**

Sampler – Design 6

		Skeins	DMC	Anchor	Madeira
	Red	I	816	1005	0512
	Pink	I	316	1017	0809
	Dark olive green	I	730	924	1614
	Mid olive green	I	732	281	1613
	Light olive green	I	734	280	1610
	Yellow	I	725	305	0106
	Cream	I	677	886	2207
	Blue	I	799	145	0910
	Brown	I	839	1050	1913

Design 7

Follow Fig 8.19. The design for this sampler is based on an original signed 'Elizabeth Bates, 10 years', and is dated 1801. This project (Fig 8.18) shows a shepherdess and lamb with a grassy hill and trees at the lower edge.

Fig 8.18 **Sampler, Design 7.**

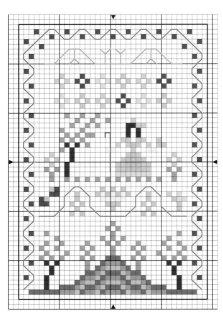

Fig 8.19 **Chart for sampler, Design 7.**

Sampler – Design 7

		Skeins	DMC	Anchor	Madeira
	Dark olive green	I	730	924	1614
	Mid olive green	I	732	281	1613
	Light olive green	I	734	280	1610
	Blue green	I	502	876	1703
	Brown	I	839	1050	1913
	Red	I	816	1005	0512
	Dark peach	I	352	9	0303
	Light peach	I	754	1012	0305
	Blue	I	799	145	0910
	Yellow	I	725	305	0106
	Cream	I	677	886	2207

Design 8

Follow Fig 8.21. The original is signed 'R Benjamin' and is undated.
The style indicates the early nineteenth century. This sampler shows
garden pavilions, tree and plant motifs, and butterflies.

Fig 8.20 **Sampler, Design 8.**

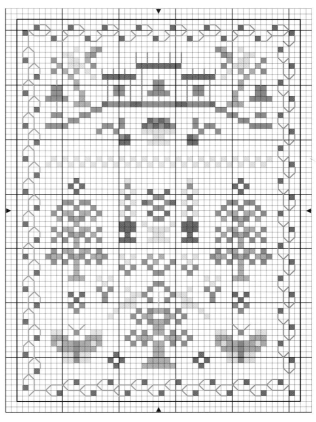

Fig 8.21 **Chart for sampler, Design 8.**

Sampler – Design 8

		Skeins	DMC	Anchor	Madeira
	Dark green	1	319	683	1313
	Red	1	816	1005	0512
	Blue	1	799	145	0910
	Brown	1	435	1046	2010

Design 9

Follow Fig 8.23. Dated 1841, the original is signed 'Elizabeth Wade, 13 years old'. The main motifs used here are plants in pots and peacocks (Fig 8.22).

Fig 8.22 **Sampler, Design 9.**

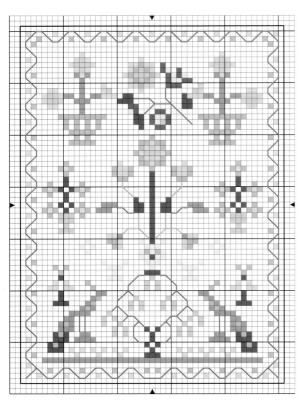

Fig 8.23 **Chart for sampler, Design 9.**

Sampler – Design 9

		Skeins	DMC	Anchor	Madeira
	Light green	1	3053	260	1603
	Dark green	1	3051	268	1508
	Light pink	1	3326	36	0606
	Dark pink	1	335	38	0610
	Light blue	1	827	9159	1014
	Dark blue	1	798	137	0911
	Yellow	1	3046	887	2206

Mounting and framing pictures and samplers

Miniature picture frame moulding comes in various sizes and some have a rebate on the reverse side to receive the mounted picture. The steps in making the frame are the same for mouldings with or without a rebate, but mounting the embroidered picture differs slightly depending on whether a rebated or flat-backed moulding is used.

Making the frame

1 Cut and mitre the moulding to the required size as shown in Fig 8.24A. The inner edges, a–a and b–b, are the same length as the outer edges of the embroidered pictures.

2 Carefully glue the sections of the frame together at the corners. Wipe away any excess glue. Allow to dry completely.

3 Stain and varnish as desired.

Mounting using rebated moulding

1 Cut a piece of mounting card to fit inside the rebate of the frame (*see* Fig 8.24B).

2 Cover the front of the card with a thin layer of PVA glue, wiping off any excess so the card is just tacky. This is very easy if the straight edge of a piece of card is drawn over the surface, leaving a uniform layer.

3 Place the embroidery into position centrally on the tacky card. Check that the position is correct and gently press down all over (*see* Fig 8.24C). Leave to dry completely.

4 Trim away the excess fabric from around the edge with a craft knife or pointed scissors.

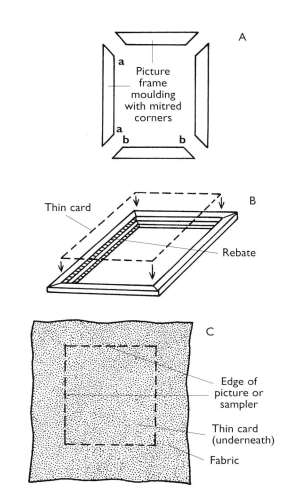

Fig 8.24 **Mounting a picture in rebated moulding.**

5 Push the picture into the frame and seal the edges on the back with narrow masking tape.

Mounting using flat-backed moulding

1 Cut a piece of mounting card 100mm (4in) square and cover it with PVA glue as described in step 2 above.

2 Place the embroidery lightly onto the tacky surface and lay the frame over it to make sure the embroidery is square. If not, gently push the embroidery into the correct position and then press down firmly. Allow to dry completely.

3 Glue the frame into position around the edge of the embroidery. Use the glue very sparingly, as it must not spread onto the embroidered surface (*see* Fig 8.25). Leave to dry completely.

4 With a sharp craft knife, cut away the surplus card and fabric from around the four sides.

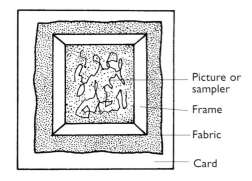

Picture or sampler

Frame

Fabric

Card

Fig 8.25 **Mounting a picture in moulding with no rebate.**

9 Bed hangings and bedcovers

During the eighteenth century the bed was important as a symbol of wealth. At the beginning of the century guests continued to be received in the bedroom. The hangings were highly decorated with rich fabrics or embroidery. The four-poster or half-tester were still fashionable, although they were much lighter and airier than in the previous centuries.

Later, a day bed was introduced, which would be placed at the foot of the main bed. This, the forerunner of the chaise longue and sofa, was eventually placed in a separate reception room where meetings would take place.

A set of hangings for a bed was a very costly outlay, with a considerable amount of fabric and labour being involved. There was a headpiece which hung above the headboard; a tester, under the canopy of the four-poster bed; upper valances around the top of the bed frame; lower valances to cover the space between the mattress and the floor; and finally, a set of two or four curtains.

This chapter contains designs for two sets of hangings for a four-poster bed, together with additional bedcovers using a variety of techniques, and basic bedding.

Bed sizes varied a great deal in Georgian times, each bed being made for the person who was going to use it. The standard bed only came with the development of mass-production methods in the later nineteenth century. Similarly, miniature beds by different makers will vary slightly in size and you will need to adjust your patterns accordingly.

Bed hangings

Determining size

To make paper patterns for bed hangings, follow the relevant instructions below and refer to Fig 9.1.

Headpiece: Measure the width between the bedposts at the head of the bed (A–B). Then measure the height from the top of the bed frame to just above the mattress or headboard level (B–G). Add 15mm (½in) all round the edges for turnings.

Tester: Measure the width (A–B) and length (A–C) of the bed inside the upper bed frame. Add 15mm (½in) all round the edges for turnings.

Upper valance: Measure the length of the side of the bed at the top of the bed frame (A–C). Continue to measure across the width (C–D) and back along the other side (D–B). The valance should be between 25 and 30mm (1 and 1¼in) wide. Add 15mm (½in) along the edges and ends for turnings.

If preferred, this upper valance can be made in three parts by having a join at each corner. In this case, 15mm (½in) turnings will be required on all three pieces, as with the lower valances.

Lower valances: Measure two pieces the length of the side of the bed between the bedposts (A–C) by the height of the mattress base (E–F). Measure one piece the width of the bed between the bedposts (C–D) by the height of the mattress base (E–F). Allow 15mm (1½in) turnings on all sides.

The curtains will be about 75mm (3in) wide and the height of the bed (C–E) with 15mm (½in) turnings on all sides.

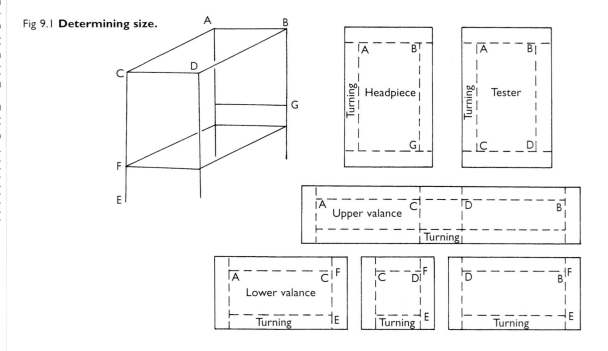

Fig 9.1 **Determining size.**

Fig 9.2 **Ribbon and Rose bed hangings.**

Ribbon and Rose Bed Hangings

The design for this project (*see* Figs 9.2 and 9.3) reflects a popular theme of the eighteenth century – floral motifs linked with ribbons and bows. Although most commonly found as surface embroidery in silk, the design has been interpreted here as a counted thread technique.

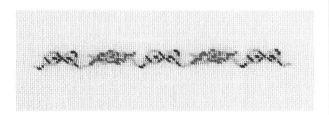

Fig 9.3 **Detail of embroidered design.**

Ribbon and Rose Bed Hangings

Materials

Evenweave linen or cotton (27, 32 or 35 count): 60cm (24in) square

Stranded cotton as listed in colour key

Tapestry needle: No. 26 or 28

Tacking cotton

Sewing thread to match fabric OR

PVA fabric glue

Size

9 x 47 stitches per pattern repeat

Size as required, according to pattern and count used

Working method

1 Make paper patterns for all the pieces required as directed above (*see* page 110).

2 Using the paper patterns, mark the fabric with tacking stitches to show the outlines of each piece. Leave sufficient fabric between the pieces to allow for the turnings. Also mark with tacking stitches the centres of each piece.

3 Either mount the whole piece of fabric in a large rectangular stretcher frame, or place a ring frame on the piece being worked at the time.

4 Refer to the chart in Fig 9.4, to work the valances. Use two strands of stranded cotton on 27 count, or one strand on 32 or 35 count, and tent stitch throughout. Work a ribbon motif at the centre of each valance, and continue to either side until the desired length has been reached; finish with a complete motif. The number of pattern repeats will vary according to the bed size and the fabric count being used.

5 Using the same chart (Fig 9.4), work either a single motif or a row of motifs above the hem of each curtain. Alternatively, the design can be used continuously, as on the valances, and positioned up the edges of the curtains.

6 To embroider the headpiece or tester, use the chart and instructions given for the chair back and seat in Chapter 5 (*see* page 68). Centre the posy within the outlines.

7 When the embroidery is complete, remove the fabric from the frame.

8 Check the measurements again by holding the pieces against the bed. The upper valance is mounted outside the curtains and may need to be longer than you expected.

9 Withdraw one thread from the evenweave fabric along the tacking lines. This allows the linen to fold back more easily, giving a neat, flat edge.

10 Make up the hangings as shown on page 116.

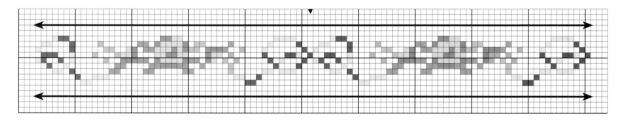

Fig 9.4 **Chart for Ribbon and Rose bed hangings.**

Ribbon and Rose Bed Hangings

		Skeins	DMC	Anchor	Madeira
	Dark blue	I	798	137	0911
	Light blue	I	827	9159	1014
	Dark pink	I	602	63	0702
	Light pink	I	776	24	0607
	Light green	I	472	264	1414
	Dark green	I	470	266	1410
	Mauve	I	554	96	0711

Fig 9.5 **Crewel Work bed hangings.**

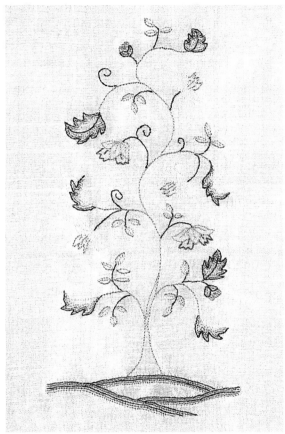

Fig 9.6 **Detail of Crewel Work design.**

Crewel Work Bed Hangings

This design reflects the popular fashion for crewel work that continued into the eighteenth century. Whereas in the previous century the style for crewel work had been large and heavy, the early Georgian period brought a light, airy treatment of the Tree of Life motif (*see* Figs 9.5 and 9.6).

Crewel Work Bed Hangings

Materials

Cream-coloured lightweight silk or cotton fabric: 60cm (24in) square

Stranded cotton as listed in colour key

Embroidery needle: No. 10

Tacking cotton

Sewing cotton to match fabric OR

PVA fabric glue

Size

As required

113

Working method

1 Make paper patterns for all the pieces required as indicated on page 110.

2 Using the paper patterns, prepare the fabric by marking the outlines of each piece with a line of tacking. Leave enough fabric between the pieces to allow for turnings.

3 Refer to the pattern in Fig 9.7, and transfer the design onto the fabric. This can be done using the tracing method, or with dressmakers'

Fig 9.7 **Pattern for Crewel Work bed hangings.**

Fig 9.8 **Stitch pattern for Crewel Work bed hangings.**

Crewel Work Bed Hangings

		Skeins	DMC	Anchor	Madeira
	Dark green	I	319	683	1313
	Mid green	I	320	216	1311
	Yellow green	I	734	280	1610
	Dark blue	I	824	132	1010
	Light blue	I	799	145	0910
	Red	I	816	1005	0512
	Peach	I	352	9	0303
	Gold	I	680	907	2210
	Yellow	I	744	301	0110

carbon, or by ironing off a photocopy. Remember that photocopying will reverse the design. (*See* Chapter 14.) The main design is placed on the curtains and the long, narrow strip is repeated for the valances. The main design can be used for a headpiece or tester by copying the upper part only.

4 Mount the fabric in an embroidery frame as for the previous project.

5 Using the colour guide and stitch diagram in Fig 9.8, work the embroidery using one strand of stranded cotton and backstitch throughout.

It is possible to begin with a tiny knot. When an area of stitching has been worked, start and finish a thread in the back of the stitching. Try to keep the back of the stitching, particularly on the curtains, as neat as possible. The stitches and colours for the leaves on the valance are the same as those shown for the main design.

6 When you have completed the embroidery, remove it from the frame. Press the embroidery, if necessary, from the reverse side, on a soft surface.

7 Make up the hangings as instructed below.

Making up bed hangings

Check that all pieces fit before trimming them to size. This is particularly important for the upper valance, as it fits over the tops of the curtains and may need to be longer than imagined. For all the following instructions, refer to Fig 9.9.

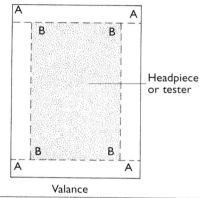

Fig 9.9
Making up bed hangings for a four-poster bed.

Headpiece or tester

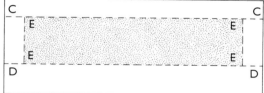

Valance

Headpiece or tester

1 Trim the edges to give a turning of 10mm (⅜in).
2 Fold the side edges under (along lines B-B) and either turn a hem and stitch, or glue using a PVA fabric glue very sparingly.
3 Fold the top edge and lower hem under (along lines A-A), and secure as above.
4 To fit a headpiece to the bed, place a fine line of glue along the top of the bed frame (A–B in Fig 9.1) and lay the top edge of the headpiece in position. Allow to dry.
5 To fit a tester, place a fine line of glue around the top edges of the bed frame

(A–B–D–C–A in Fig 9.1). Place the tester into position and allow to dry.

Lower valances

1 Trim the edges to give a turning of 15mm (½in).
2 Fold under the two short ends (along lines E-E) and secure as above with stitches or glue.
3 Fold under the top and lower edges (along lines C-C and D-D), and secure.
4 To fit the lower valances, place a thin line of glue along the mattress support at the sides and foot of the bed. Place the individual valances into position and allow to dry.

Curtains

1 Make and pleat the curtains as indicated for window curtains in Chapter 4 (*see* page 40). Allow 15mm (½in) hem at the lower edge.
2 When the gathering threads have been removed, or the fabric is removed from the pleater, cut the curtains to the height of the bed (E–C in Fig 9.1).
3 To fit the bed curtains, place a little glue along the reverse side of the upper edge of the gathered curtain, and place it into position on the outer edge of the bed frame.

Upper valance

1 Whether the upper valance is in one or three pieces, turn the short ends under and secure with stitches or glue.
2 Turn under and secure the top and lower hems.
3 To fit the upper valance(s), place a thin line of glue around the outer edge of the upper bed frame and attach the upper valance(s). Allow to dry.

Bedcovers

Determining size

A bedcover can be made to extend down to floor level or to cover only the top surface of the bed. To determine the exact size required, place the mattress and any bedding on the bed. This will allow the complete drop to be measured, i.e., the height from the floor to the top edge of the bedding and mattress.

A bedcover or quilt to cover the top of the bed only should match the width and length of the bed (a–b and b–c in Fig 9.10C).

A bedcover with a drop to the floor has the height to the top edge of the bedding added (*see* Fig 9.10A). If the bed is a four-poster or has bedposts at the foot, the corners of the bedcover will need to be omitted (*see* Fig 9.10B).

The patterns for the following projects can be adjusted to give an accurate fit, either by adding to the edges or by reducing the pattern

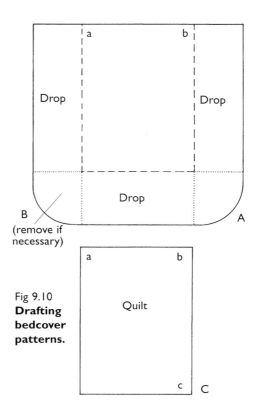

Fig 9.10
Drafting bedcover patterns.

on a photocopier. A wide choice of techniques has been used for the projects – crewel work, flat quilting, wadded quilting, and pieced and simulated patchwork.

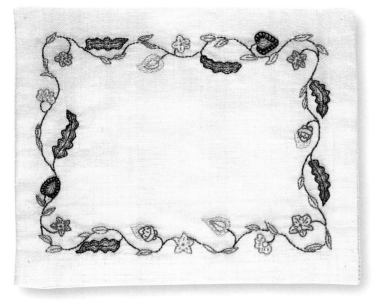

Fig 9.11
Crewel Work bedcover.

Crewel Work Bedcover

The design for this crewel work bedcover is based on a curtain from the first quarter of the eighteenth century.

Crewel Work Bedcover

Materials

Lightweight silk or cotton fabric: 200 x 300mm (8 x 12in)

Stranded cotton as listed in colour key

Embroidery needle: No. 10

Sewing thread to match fabric

Size

135 x 110mm (5⅜ x 4½in) or as required

Working method

1 Make a paper pattern to the desired size (*see* Fig 9.10). Allow a turning of 15–20mm (½–¾in) on each edge.

2 Cut the fabric into two pieces, each 200 x 150mm (8 x 6in). Mark the outline of the bedcover on one piece of the fabric with a tacking line. The second piece of fabric is the lining for the bedcover.

3 Transfer the pattern in Fig 9.12 onto the fabric using the tracing method, or dressmakers' carbon, or by ironing off a photocopy. Remember that the photocopy method will reverse the design. Details of these methods can be found in Chapter 14.

4 Mount the fabric in a small round or rectangular frame (*see* Chapter 13).

5 Refer to the stitch and colour guide in Fig 9.13 and work the embroidery using one strand of stranded cotton. The two dark blue flowers are edged with blanket stitch.

Fig 9.12 **Pattern for Crewel Work bedcover.**

Crewel Work Bedcover

		Skeins	DMC	Anchor	Madeira
	Bright pink	I	892	28	0412
	Light pink	I	894	26	0414
	Dark red	I	816	1005	0512
	Red	I	321	47	0510
	Dark blue	I	823	152	1008
	Mid blue	I	517	169	1107
	Light blue	I	807	168	1109
	Dark green	I	319	683	1313
	Light green	I	320	216	1311

Fig 9.13 **Stitch pattern for Crewel Work bedcover.**

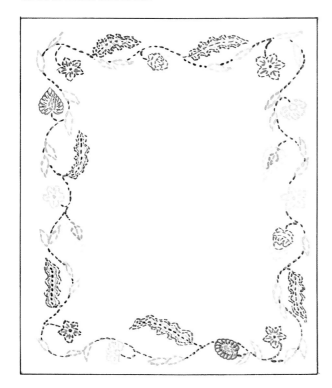

Some flowers have small straight stitches inside, and the rest of the embroidery is in backstitch.

6 Begin with a tiny knot, and after that begin and end a thread by working it into the back of existing stitchery.

7 When the embroidery is complete, remove it from the frame. Press if necessary, from the reverse side on a soft surface. Make up as follows.

8 Trim the turnings of the bedcover to 10mm (⅜in), and cut the lining to the same size.

9 Turn under the edges of both pieces as shown in Fig 9.14.

10 Place the two pieces with the reverse faces together and stitch the edges together.

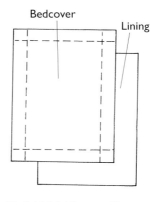
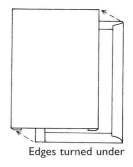

Fig 9.14 **Making up the Crewel Work bedcover.**

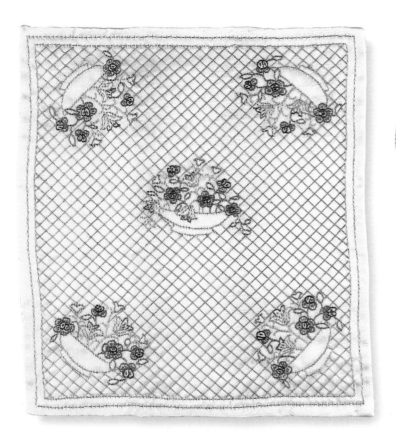

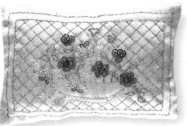

Fig 9.15 **Gold bedcover and pillow.**

Gold Bedcover and Pillow

Quilting reached a height of popularity and quality during the eighteenth century. Wadded quilting, also known as English, Durham and miners' quilting, consists of three layers; the top fabric, wadding and a backing fabric. The three layers are stitched through to provide a warm, soft covering.

Corded quilting, also known as Italian, has only two layers of fabric. The design is formed of parallel stitched lines which provide a channel through which quilting wool is threaded.

Gold Bedcover and Pillow

Materials

Cream-coloured satin: 200 x 180mm (8 x 7in) + 80 x 200mm (3⅛ x 8in)

Lightweight silk or cotton: 200 x 180mm (8 x 7in)

Stranded cotton and metallic thread as listed in colour key

Embroidery needle: No. 10

Sewing thread in old gold or mustard

Sewing thread to match fabric

Size

Bedcover

155 x 135mm (6⅛ x 5⅜in) or as required

Pillow

50 x 70mm (2 x 2¾in)

Stuffed quilting, or Trapunto, is also made from two layers of fabric. Only selective areas are padded, by pushing wadding through from the reverse side.

Flat quilting was a technique peculiar to the eighteenth century. Consisting of two layers of fabric, this method did not use any form of padding. It was used for magnificent sets of bedcovers, bolsters and pillows, produced

Fig 9.16
Patterns for Gold bedcover and pillow.

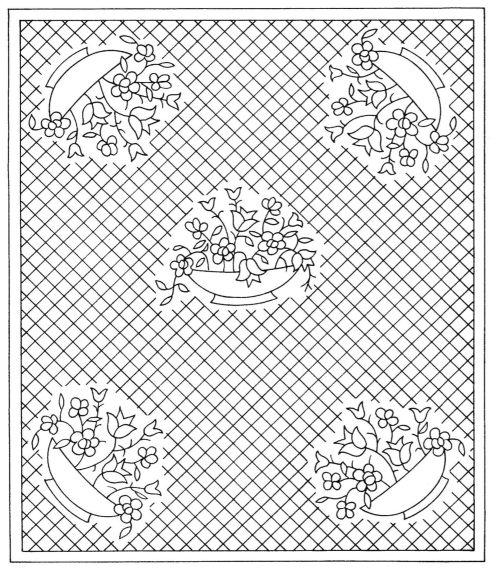

mainly in professional workshops as prestigious wedding gifts. The finest examples had an all-over pattern, which often mimicked traditional quilting patterns, stitched with gold or silver gilt metal threads. Areas of beautifully coloured silk embroidery added to the richness, often featuring gold bowls or baskets of naturalistic flowers.

The design for this project (*see* Fig 9.15) is based on one such set of elaborate flat quilting, dated 1717, in the Bowes Museum in County Durham. Some excellent examples can also be seen in the Victoria and Albert Museum in London.

Working method

1 Transfer the pattern from Fig 9.16 onto the fabric. Use one of the following methods: tracing through the fabric, dressmakers' carbon, or iron a photocopy off onto the satin fabric. The last method will reverse the design (*see* Chapter 14).

2 Mount the fabric into a rectangular frame.

3 Referring to the stitch pattern and colour guide in Fig 9.17 and work all the coloured embroidery in one strand of stranded cotton using backstitch throughout.

Fig 9.17
Stitch pattern for Gold bedcover and pillow.

Gold Bedcover and Pillow

		Skeins	DMC	Anchor	Madeira
	Dark green	1	470	266	1410
	Light green	1	472	264	1414
	Dark red	1	815	43	0512
	Light red	1	321	47	0510
	Dark mauve	1	553	99	0712
	Light mauve	1	554	96	0711
	Blue	1	799	145	0910
	Metallic Gold	1	Fil d'Or	–	No. 40

Fig 9.18 **Working the trellis.**

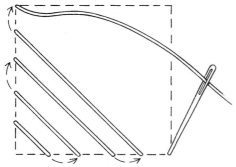

Working the first layer of
diagonal threads

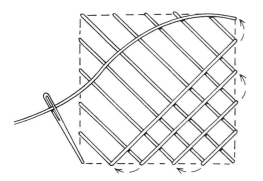

Placing the second layer of threads

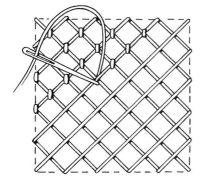

Stitching over each crossing point

4 Work the flower bowls in metallic thread using backstitch.

5 Using the lines of the background trellis, lay the metallic threads as shown in Fig 9.18. Thread the needle with metallic thread and bring to the front, at the end of one of the trellis lines. Take the needle down through the fabric at the other end of the line. Lay all the diagonal threads in one direction first.

6 Lay the second layer of threads along the opposite diagonal lines.

7 With the old gold or mustard coloured sewing thread, work along the lines of the trellis placing a tiny stitch over the places where the laid threads cross (*see* Fig 9.18).

8 Place the piece of lining fabric onto the back of the embroidered bedcover and hold in place by tacking around the edge outside the design. (This step is not required for the pillow.)

9 Now work the inner line around the edge of the trellis with metallic thread in backstitch. Leave the outer line, as this is worked after the edge of the bedcover has been turned. (The outer line can be worked on the pillow.)

10 Remove the piece from the embroidery frame.

11 For the bedcover, trim the turnings of the fabric and lining around the edges to 10mm (⅜in) outside the design line. Turn both edges to the inside, rather like the Crewel work bedcover (*see* Fig 9.14), and stitch the edge. Finally, work the remaining row of backstitch in metallic thread through the last line of the design.

12 For the pillows, make up and fill as instructed for a cushion in Chapter 5 (*see* pages 63 and 64).

Quilted bedcovers

Two quilted bedcover designs are included here, both suited to the whole of the eighteenth century and into the nineteenth. It is essential to use a soft fabric when quilting in miniature.

Silk, crêpe-backed satin, cotton lawn or voile are ideal. Either domette or layers of muslin are suitable as a substitute for wadding, which is usually too thick for miniature work.

Vine Bedcover

This bedcover features a grape and vine motif in the centre, with fans and scallop shells in the corners.

Fig 9.19 **Vine bedcover.**

Vine Bedcover

Materials

Lightweight soft fabric: 240 x 200mm (9½ x 8in)

Domette: 240 x 200mm (9½ x 8in) OR

Muslin: 240 x 200mm (9½ x 8in) x 4

Habutai silk lining: 240 x 200mm (9½ x 8in)

Sewing or quilting thread to match fabric

Quilting needle: No. 10

Tacking thread

Size

185 x 160mm (7¼ x 6¼in) or as required

Fig 9.20 **Feather and Fan bedcover.**

Feather and Fan Bedcover

The central design in this bedcover is based on the traditional feather motif. The fan shape placed in each corner was another popular motif of the time. It is also used in the Vine Bedcover opposite.

Working method for quilted bedcovers

1 Photocopy the pattern you have chosen from Fig 9.21 or 9.22.

2 Iron the photocopy off onto the Habutai lining. Details of this process are given in Chapter 14 (*see* page 167).

Feather and Fan Bedcover

Materials

Lightweight soft fabric: 200mm (8in) square

Domette: 200mm (8in) square OR

Muslin: 200mm (8in) square

Habutai silk lining: 200mm (8in) square

Sewing or quilting thread to match fabric

Quilting needle: No. 10

Tacking thread

Size

160mm (6¼in) square

Fig 9.21 **Pattern for Vine bedcover.**

Fig 9.22 **Pattern for Feather and Fan bedcover.**

3 Press all fabric to remove creases.

4 Assemble the fabrics ready for quilting. Place the Habutai silk design side down onto the work surface. Lay the domette or muslin layers on the Habutai. Lay the bedcover fabric on top, right side up (*see* Fig 9.23).

5 Using tacking cotton, secure the 'sandwich' of fabrics together with large tacking stitches all over.

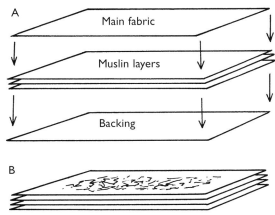

Fig 9.23 **Assembling fabrics for quilting.**

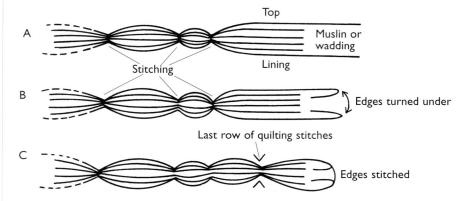

Fig 9.24 **Finishing the edges of quilted bedcovers.**

6 Begin to stitch the design, working from the centre. Use the matching sewing or quilting thread with a small running stitch. A smaller stitch can be achieved by stab stitching rather than trying to make more than one stitch at a time.

7 Continue to stitch the design, gradually working towards the outside edges. Do not work the line that forms the very outside edge of the design, as this forms part of the making-up process.

8 To finish the edges, trim the domette or muslin layers back to the stitching (*see* Fig 9.24). Trim the fabric and lining to 10mm (⅜in) around the edges. Turn the edges inside and stitch together.

9 Finally, work the remaining outside line of quilting to give a neat edge.

Patchwork Bedcovers

Many of the traditional patterns for pieced patchwork would be suitable for a Georgian dolls' house. When making patchwork on a miniature scale, one of the secrets of success is in the choice of fabric. Only lightweight fabric woven with natural fibres should be used, i.e., pure silk and cotton lawn or voile. Do not mix more than one type of fabric together.

Another tip is to have a generous seam allowance while the pieces are being put together, and to press the seam open before cutting the seam allowance down to about 2mm (¹⁄₁₆in). For the projects in this section I have quoted seam allowances of 6mm (¼in), which are, in some cases, wider than the pieces being joined. These turnings are then cut away after pressing, making it easier to handle and giving a beautifully flat seam.

Two very simple designs are given for the pieced patchwork, and two further, more complex, designs are shown as simulated patchwork. It is also possible to use commercially printed fabric to simulate pieced patchwork.

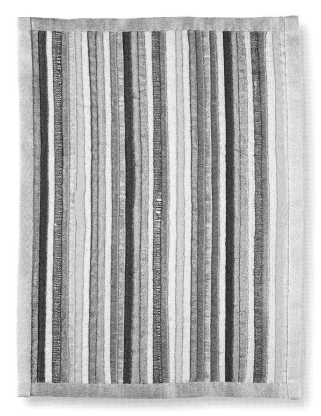

Fig 9.25 **Strip
Patchwork bedcover.**

cover shown in Fig 9.25 is made with pure silk fabric, which gives a softer finish than the cotton used for the cushion.

Working method

1 Take a photocopy of the pattern in Fig 9.26. This can be enlarged if desired.

2 Iron the photocopy off onto the Habutai silk. The stitching will be worked from this, the reverse side of the bedcover.

3 Cut the pieces of lightweight fabric into strips 25mm wide and 200mm long (1 x 8in). The strips can be two, three or four colours repeated, or as many colours as desired.

4 Lay the first strip of fabric on the Habutai,

Strip Patchwork Bedcover

This bedcover is assembled using the same method as the cushion shown in Chapter 5 (*see* page 59). The silk strips are mounted on a base fabric of Habutai silk and the edge of this bedcover is bound with strips of fabric. The

Strip Patchwork Bedcover

Materials

Habutai silk lining: 200 x 180mm (8 x 7in)

Selection of lightweight fabric strips (silk, cotton lawn or voile):

   25 x 200mm (1 x 8in)

Sewing thread

Quilting needle: No. 10

Size

170 x 125mm (6¾ x 5in)

Fig 9.26 **Pattern for Strip Patchwork bedcover.**

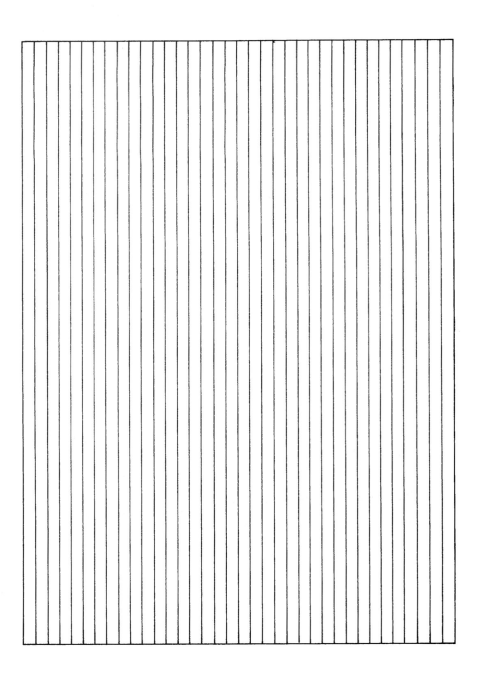

on the side of the fabric without the photocopy (*see* Fig 9.27A). It is possible to see through the Habutai to check the position of the fabric.

5 From the photocopied side of the Habutai (the reverse side of bedcover) hand or machine stitch along the line of the pattern.

6 Trim the seam allowance away, then fold over and press (*see* Fig 9.27B and C).

7 Continue to add the strips in the same way until the whole bedcover is filled (*see* Fig 9.27D).

8 Cut a strip of fabric 30mm (1¼in) wide to fit the top and lower edges of the bedcover (*see*

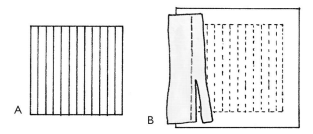
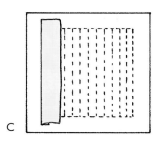
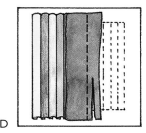

A   B   C   D

Fig 9.27 **Assembling the Strip Patchwork bedcover.**

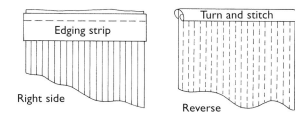

Edging strip

Right side

Turn and stitch

Reverse

Fig 9.28 **Making up the Strip Patchwork bedcover.**

Fig 9.29 **Simple Squares Patchwork bedcover.**

Fig 9.28). Hand or machine stitch it into place on the right side of the bedcover as shown.

9 Fold the strip over the edge of the bedcover. Trim away any excess fabric if necessary.

10 Tuck the edge under and then hand stitch into place.

11 Repeat this process with strips of fabric along the two sides of the bedcover.

Simple Squares Patchwork Bedcover

This bedcover (*see* Fig 9.29) is assembled in the same way as the cushion shown on page 60. Lightweight cotton or silk fabric is ideal.

Working method

1 Refer to Fig 9.30 and join the strips by machine stitching into pairs initially, with a seam allowance of 6mm (¼in).

2 Press the seam open and trim the allowance down to 2mm (1/16in). (*See* Fig 9.30B.)

3 Continue joining the resulting strips, pressing the seams and trimming as you go, until all the strips are joined. (*See* Fig 9.30C.)

4 Cut across the strips at 18mm (¾in) intervals. This will give 30 strips.

Simple Squares Patchwork Bedcover

Materials

Fabric strips: 18 x 550mm (¾ x 22in) x 30

Lining fabric: 200mm (8in) square

Sewing thread

Sewing machine

Embroidery needle: No. 10

NB: The quantity of fabric quoted is for a bedcover
180mm (7in) square (30 x 30 squares).

Size

As required – the finished size
of each square is 6mm (¼in)

Fig 9.30 **Assembling the Simple Squares bedcover.**

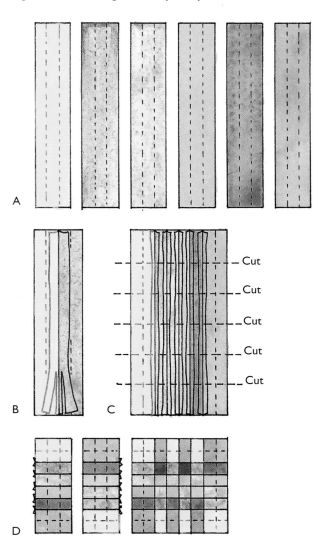

5 Alternate the strips 'top to tail' and proceed to join these strips in the same manner as above, initially in pairs. Press and trim the seams as you go.

6 When all the squares are joined, make up the bedcover in the same way as the Crewel Work bedcover (*see* page 119, steps 8–11). Turn the edges of the front and lining of the bedcover as shown in Fig 9.14. Place the two reverse sides together and hand stitch the edges.

7 The bedcover can be 'tied' if desired (*see* Fig 9.31). Using sewing cotton, pick up a small amount of fabric with the needle at the corner of a square, passing through both layers of the bedcover. Draw the needle through, leaving an end of thread. Cut the needle and thread off, leaving another end of thread. Tie the two ends in a knot and trim the excess thread away.

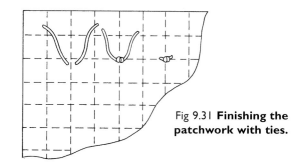

Fig 9.31 **Finishing the patchwork with ties.**

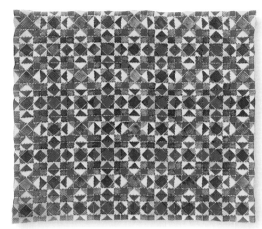

Fig 9.32 Above
**Geometric Block
bedcover.**

Fig 9.33 **Flower
Basket bedcover.**

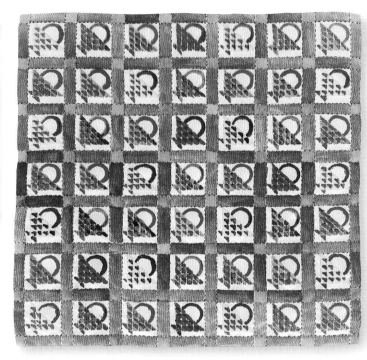

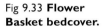

Simulated Patchwork Bedcovers

This is a very good method for creating miniature patchwork that is true to scale. Any design, however detailed, can be reproduced. Two block patterns are given here, one geometric and one showing a traditional flower basket (*see* Figs 9.32 and 9.33).

Working method

1 Photocopy the desired pattern from Figs 9.34 and 9.35, or use your own design.

2 Colour the photocopy with the fabric transfer paints. Details of this process are given in Chapter 15 (*see* page 170).

3 Iron the coloured copy onto the fabric, making sure that the design is on the straight grain of the fabric.

Simulated Patchwork Bedcovers

Materials

Lightweight synthetic fabric (satin, crêpe de Chine, lining, etc.): 220mm (8⅝in) square

Lining fabric: 220mm (8⅝in) square

Muslin: 220mm (8⅝in) square x 2

Fabric transfer paints in desired colours

Sewing thread to match dominant colour

Quilting needle: No. 10

Size

As required

Fig 9.34 **Pattern for Geometric Block bedcover.**

4 The impression of piecing is given by lightly quilting the main lines of the pattern. To achieve this, place the coloured fabric on top of the layers of muslin with the lining underneath, as shown in Fig 9.23 on page 127.

5 Hold the layers together with tacking stitches.

6 Using a small running stitch, quilt the layers together along the main lines of the pattern.

7 Finish the edges using the same method as shown for the quilted bedcovers (*see* Fig 9.24).

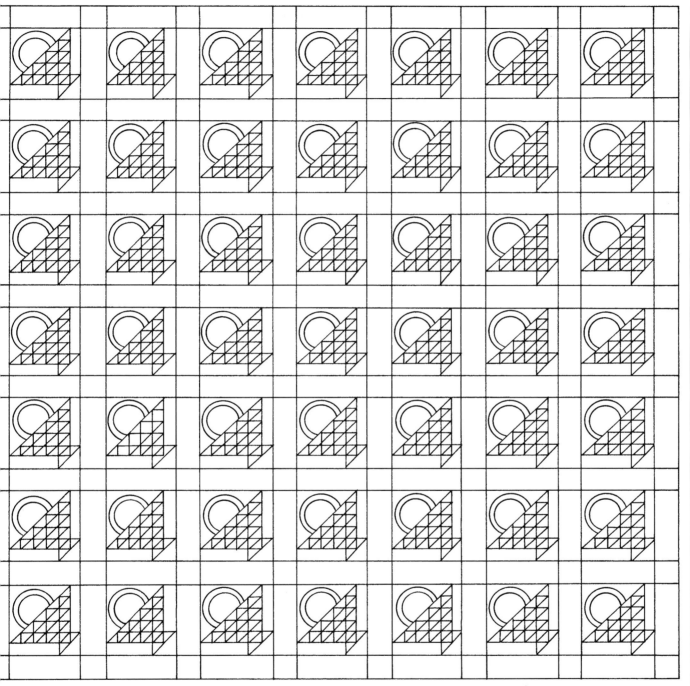

Fig 9.35 **Pattern for Flower Basket bedcover.**

Bedding

Although they are often covered by bedcovers and hangings, you will still need a mattress and pillow. You may also like to complete the bedclothes by adding sheets and blankets.

Mattresses

The early mattresses were simple bags that were filled with any soft filling that was available – straw, animal fibres, feathers, etc. Later mattresses, especially with the advent of springs, required a box edge.

When making miniature mattresses or pillows, do not be tempted to overfill them. By the time the remaining covers are in place the bed can look out of scale. It is also a good idea to make the mattress a little smaller than the actual bed to allow for the covers.

Working methods

Early Mattress

1 Make a paper pattern as shown in Fig 9.36A: a–b = desired width; b–c = desired length. Add 6mm (¼in) all round for the seam.

2 Cut two pieces of fabric to the paper pattern.

3 Place the fabric, right sides together, and stitch around the seam line by hand or machine. Leave an opening at one end (*see* Fig 9.36B).

4 Turn the mattress to the right side and fill as desired. Wadding or cotton wool will give a soft, padded effect. If you desire a 'lived-in' look, stuff the mattress nearly full with small plastic beads.

5 Sew up the opening.

6 The mattress can be given a buttoned effect by taking a thread through it, then back, and knotting the ends (*see* Fig 9.36D). Cut the two ends, leaving a tuft of thread.

Mattress

Materials

For early mattress
Cotton, linen or fine scrim

For later mattress
Lightweight calico or cotton with a narrow stripe

For both mattresses
Wadding, cotton wool or small beads
Sewing cotton
Sewing needles

Size

To find the size required, measure the width and length of the bed. Deduct 10mm (⅜in) from the width and 6mm (¼in) from the length

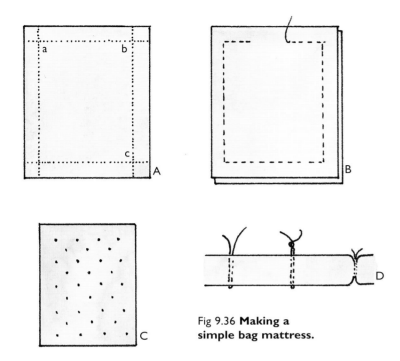

Fig 9.36 **Making a simple bag mattress.**

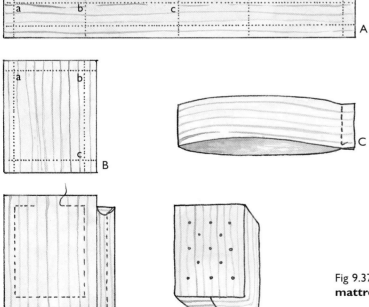

Fig 9.37 **Making a mattress with a gusset.**

Later Mattress

1 Make a paper pattern, as above, and cut two pieces of fabric (*see* Fig 9.37B).

2 Cut a fabric gusset long enough to fit around the edge of the mattress, i.e., twice the width plus twice the length plus 12mm (½in) turning (*see* Fig 9.37A).

3 Fold the gusset in half and seam the short ends together (*see* Fig 9.37C).

4 Carefully pin the gusset into position on one of the main pieces of fabric (*see* Fig 9.37D) and stitch by hand or machine.

5 Repeat the last stage with the second piece of fabric, but this time leave an opening when stitching.

6 Turn through to the right side, fill the mattress and sew up the opening as above.

7 Tie if desired.

Pillows and Bolsters

The standard size of most pillows is 74 x 48cm (29 x 19in), giving a miniature scale of 60 x 40mm (2⅜ x 1⁹⁄₁₆in). A bolster should be long enough to fit the width of the bed.

Working method

1 Cut two pieces of cotton lawn or handkerchief fabric 70 x 50mm (2¾ x 2in) for a pillow or about 10mm longer than the width of the bed x 50mm (2in) for a bolster. Stitch the pieces together by hand or machine with a seam allowance of 5mm (³⁄₁₆in). Leave an opening at one end (*see* Fig 9.38A).

2 Turn through to the right side.

3 Fill as advised for mattresses, above.

4 Turn the allowance at the open end in and stitch across the end of the pillow or bolster (*see* Fig 9.38B and C).

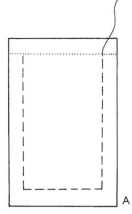

Fig 9.38 **Making a pillowcase.**

A

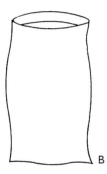

B

C

Pillows and Bolsters

Materials

Cotton lawn or handkerchief fabric: 70 x 50mm (2¾ x 2in) x 2

Wadding, cotton wool or small beads

Sewing cotton

Sewing needles

Size

60 x 40mm (2⅜ x 1⁹⁄₁₆in) or as required

Bed linen

Pillowcase

Working method

1 Cut two pieces of cotton lawn or handkerchief fabric as for the pillow, but 10mm (⅜in) larger.
2 Make up as for the pillow but do not stitch up the opening.
3 Tuck the allowance around the opening inside, and work a row of running stitches to hold it in place.
4 Place the pillowcase on the pillow.

Sheets

Working method

1 To determine the size, refer to Fig 9.39, measure the bed and make a paper pattern. On the diagram, A–B = the width and B–C = the length of bed. Add the depth of the mattress plus 30mm (1¼in) 'tuck-in' to three sides. Add 20mm (¾in) 'turn-back' to the top of the sheet. Add 6mm (¼in) to all sides.
2 Turn a narrow hem on all sides and stitch.
3 A narrow lace edging can be added to the top edge if required.

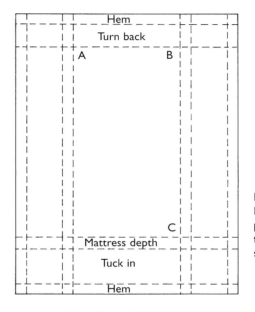

Fig 9.39 **Making a pattern for a sheet.**

Pillowcase

Materials	Size
Cotton lawn or handkerchief fabric: 10mm (⅜in) larger than pillow to be covered	As required
Sewing cotton	
Sewing needles	

Sheets

Materials	Size
Very lightweight cotton lawn, voile or a cotton handkerchief should be used for sheets as they fold well	As required
Lace, if required	
Sewing cotton	
Sewing needles	

Blankets

Working method

1 Cut the blanket to the same size as the sheet, without any hem allowance.

2 Simply decorate the top edge of the blanket with blanket stitch.

Blankets

Materials

Very lightweight wool, flannel or Vyella
Sewing cotton
Sewing needles

Size

As required

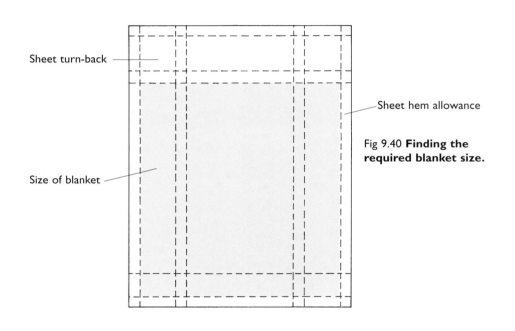

Sheet turn-back

Sheet hem allowance

Size of blanket

Fig 9.40 **Finding the required blanket size.**

10 Small decorative items

The projects in this section are a variety of items that do not really fit under the headings of the other chapters. Whereas the Victorians loved their homes to be cluttered and decorated with embroidered items of all kinds, the Georgians were rather more restrained.

Trompe l'oeil Card Table

The Georgians were fond of creating the illusion of a three-dimensional image on a perfectly flat surface. They used paint effects to give the appearance of alcoves, niches, false doorways and balconies on their walls, and extended the same principles to the design of embroidered furnishings.

In Chapter 5, two footstools featured trompe l'oeil designs. Another favourite was the gaming table. The design for this project is based on an eighteenth-century card table which can be seen in Aston Hall, Birmingham. It shows a game in progress, with a bag of coins or gaming chips and playing cards laid out. Use one strand of stranded cotton and tent stitch throughout.

The example shown in Fig 10.1 has a painted background. The linen has been coloured with fabric dye before being embroidered. This reduces the thickness of the finished piece and also the amount of work involved. The alternative methods of colouring fabric are given in Chapter 15.

Fig 10.1 **Trompe l'oeil card table.**

141

Trompe l'oeil Card Table

Materials

Evenweave linen (35 or 40 count): 120mm (5in) square

Stranded cotton as listed in colour key

Card embroidery frame

Tapestry needle: No. 26 or 28

Fabric paint, dye or watercolour paint

Stripwood, jelutong, obeche or mahogany: 3 x 75 x 75mm (⅛ x 3 x 3in)

Stripwood, jelutong, obeche or mahogany: 3 x 10 x 300mm (⅛ x ⅜ x 12in)

Miniature moulding: 300mm (12in) OR

Flat trim: 300mm (12in)

Cabriole table legs x 4

PVA wood glue

Stain and varnish if desired

Craft knife

Ruler

Size

100 x 100 stitches

40 count linen: 64mm (2½in) square

35 count linen: 73mm (2⅞in) square

NB: The sizes quoted indicate the size of the embroidered area; the finished table size will include a border (*see* Fig 10.2).

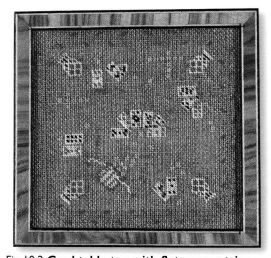

Fig 10.2 **Card table top with flat veneer trim.**

Preparation

If desired, colour the fabric as described above. Mount the fabric in the card embroidery frame as described in Chapter 13 (*see* page 163), mark the outer edges and the horizontal and vertical centres with tacking stitches.

Working method

Refer to the chart in Fig 10.3. It is possible to begin embroidering the design either in the centre or at the middle of one side. If the fabric has not been coloured, fill in the background with the colour suggested on the colour key after the design has been worked.

Making up the table top

1 If the embroidery has distorted badly, block it into shape as described in Chapter 16.

2 Cut the square table top to the required size from the 75mm (3in) square stripwood. The size will be the size of the completed embroidery plus an allowance for the moulding or flat trim (probably a total of around 75mm or 3in). Sand the edges smooth with sandpaper.

3 On the underside of the table top, measure in 10mm (⅜in) from each side and draw a line.

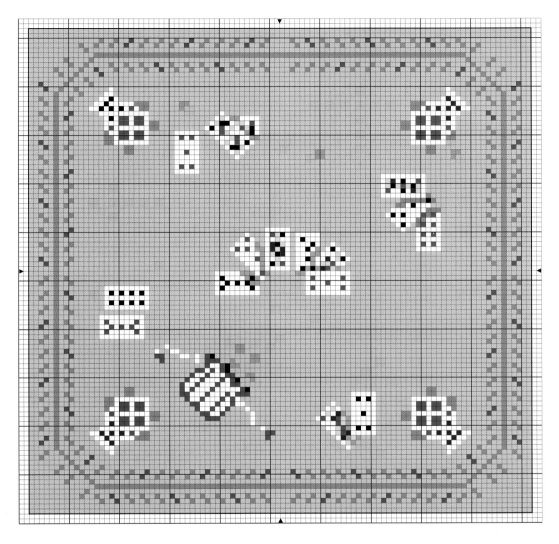

Trompe l'oeil Card Table

Fig 10.3 **Chart for Trompe l'oeil card table.**

		Skeins	DMC	Anchor	Madeira
	Green	1	502	876	1703
	Red	1	321	47	0510
	Grey	1	318	399	1802
	White	1	Blanc	White	White
	Black	1	310	Black	Black
	Yellow	1	444	297	0105
	Dark blue	1	820	134	0904
	Dark gold	1	832	907	2202
	Light gold	1	834	874	2206
	Blue	1	799	145	0910

This will give a square in the centre with a 10mm (⅜in) border around the edge. This is the guide line for the table rails and legs.

4 Cut 4 pieces of 3 x 10mm (⅛ x ⅜in) stripwood, each 45mm (1¾in) long. These are the rails which fit between and support the legs.

5 Using the drawn lines as a guide, glue the legs and rails to the underside of the table top (*see* Fig 10.4). It may be necessary to sand the legs to soften the shape. Leave to dry.

6 Stain and varnish as desired, excluding the top of the table. Leave to dry.

7 Spread PVA glue all over the top of the table, scraping off any excess.

8 Lay the embroidery into place and gently press down, making sure that the fabric is square with the table top. Allow to dry.

9 Trim any excess fabric from around the edges of the table.

Fig 10.4 **Making up the card table.**

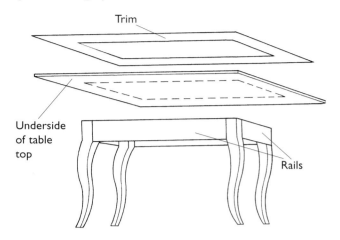

Trim

Underside of table top

Rails

10 Make a 'frame' with the moulding or flat strip, as shown for a picture frame in Chapter 8 (*see* page 107). Stain and varnish if desired.

11 When dry, glue into place around the edge of the table top, covering the edges of the fabric. Use the glue very sparingly so that it does not squeeze out onto the fabric surface.

Bell Pulls

A bell pull would have been positioned either near the fireplace, or by the door. Three designs are shown in Fig 10.5. One mimics a cord and tassel, another a tiny repeated floral motif, and the last a classical geometrical motif. They will all suit the whole of the Georgian period, so let your choice be influenced by the general decor within the room. All the designs can be repeated to achieve whatever length is needed.

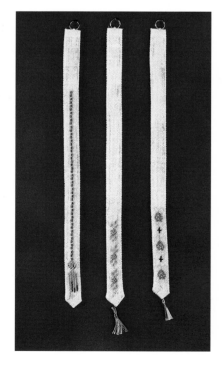

Fig 10.5
The three bell pulls.

Bell Pulls

Materials

Evenweave linen (35 count): 200 x 40mm (8 x 1½in)

Stranded cotton as listed in colour key

Tapestry needle: No. 26 or 28

Size

Each bell pull

10mm (⅜in) wide x required length

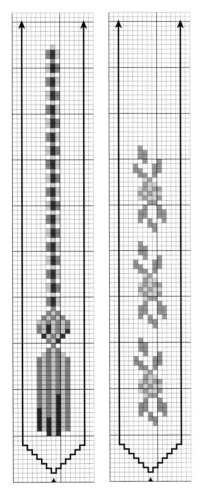

Fig 10.6
Chart for Tassel bell pull.

Fig 10.7
Chart for Roses bell pull.

Bell Pull – Tassel

		Skeins	DMC	Anchor	Madeira
	Brown	I	801	359	2007
	Gold	I	3045	888	2103
	Yellow	I	676	891	2208

Bell Pull – Roses

		Skeins	DMC	Anchor	Madeira
	Green	I	3053	260	1603
	Dark pink	I	335	38	0610
	Light pink	I	3326	36	0606

Preparation

The bell pulls can all be worked in the hand. However, if you prefer, mount the fabric into a card or ring frame. Withdraw a thread from the fabric, vertically, to mark one side edge. Leave 13 threads in, then withdraw the next thread to mark the other side edge.

Working method

Refer to the chart for your chosen design (*see* Figs 10.6, 10.7 and 10.8).

Work the design, beginning at the lower edge, leaving enough fabric (about 25mm (1in)) to form the pointed end. Use one strand of stranded cotton and tent stitch throughout.

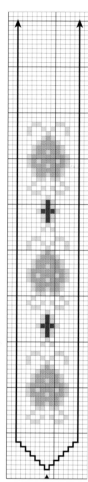

Fig 10.8
Chart for Classical bell pull.

Bell Pull – Classical

		Skeins	DMC	Anchor	Madeira
	Gold	I	725	305	0106
	Light blue	I	799	145	0910
	Dark blue	I	820	134	0904

Making up the bell pulls

Trim the side edges of the bell pull to 6mm (¼in). Shape the upper and lower edges as shown in Fig 10.9, securing with a small amount of fabric glue. Turn back and secure each side with a small amount of fabric glue.

Finally, stitch a small ring to the top. Alternatively, small decorative bell-pull fittings can be purchased from suppliers. A co-ordinating tassel can be made and stitched to the lower point.

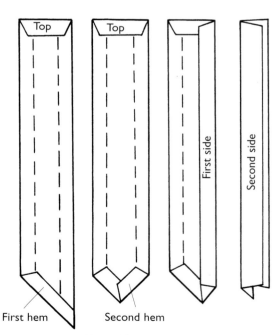

Fig 10.9
Making up the bell pulls.

Fig 10.10 **Crewel work workbags.**

Workbag

Needlework and embroidery were popular pastimes with Georgian ladies. An ongoing piece of needlework would be placed in an embroidered workbag with a drawstring top to protect it when it was not in use. These bags were usually decorated with a crewel work design on a cotton or linen twill fabric.

Preparation

Mark the outline of the bag and copy the design from Fig 10.11 onto the fabric. Use either the tracing, dressmakers' carbon or photocopy method. Remember, the photocopy method will reverse the design. (*See* Chapter 14 for details of all these methods.)

Place the fabric into a card mount or small round embroidery frame.

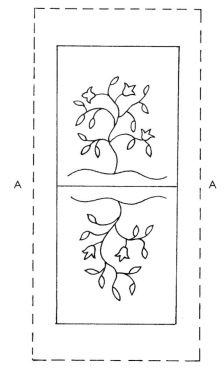

Fig 10.11 **Pattern for workbag.**

Workbag

Materials

Lightweight silk or cotton fabric: 150 x 100mm (6 x 4in)

Stranded cotton as listed in colour key

Embroidery or quilting needle: No. 10

Sewing cotton to match fabric

Size

38 x 32mm (1½ x 1¼in)

Fig 10.12 **Stitch pattern for workbag.**

Workbag

		Skeins	DMC	Anchor	Madeira
	Dark green	I	470	266	1410
	Light green	I	472	264	1414
	Red	I	321	47	0510

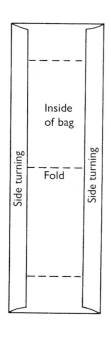

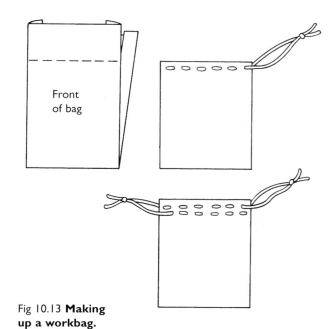

Fig 10.13 **Making up a workbag.**

Working method

Work the design in one strand of stranded cotton and backstitch throughout. Refer to the stitch and colour guide in Fig 10.12.

When complete, remove from the embroidery frame and make up as shown above, in Fig 10.13.

Making up the workbag

Fold the side turnings to the reverse side of the bag, then fold the bag along the centre horizontal line (A–A in Fig 10.11). Stitch the side edges together with sewing cotton. Next, turn the top hem down inside the bag. Using three strands of stranded cotton in the desired colour, work through the hem with a running stitch across the front and back, leaving long ends (*see* Fig 10.13).

Repeat this step, working from the opposite side, leaving long ends once again.

Tie knots in the long ends about 30mm (1¼in) from the bag, and trim the excess thread to form small tassels. Draw the threads up to close the bag (*see* Fig 10.13).

11 Wall hangings

There was a fashion during the eighteenth century for large, embroidered or tapestry woven wall hangings. These would either hang on the wall or be mounted into the panelling. The most popular designs were pastoral or garden scenes. Many examples survive in large historical houses.

Two fine canvaswork hangings (and a large collection of samplers) can be seen in Montacute House near Yeovil, Somerset. Known as the Stoke Edith hangings, they show formal Georgian garden settings and costume, and include large embroidered Chinese pots in the foreground.

A set of canvaswork hangings, c.1717, in the style of the Tree of Life, can be seen framed within panelling at Wallington Hall in Cambo, Northumberland. They were worked by Lady Julia Calverley, and reflect the heavy designs used for crewel work in the late seventeenth century.

Fig 11.1 **Conservatory wall hanging mounted within Georgian panelling.**

Conservatory Wall Hanging

Many large country houses would have had an orangery built in the grounds to house exotic fruit and plants, and to provide a place to walk in bad weather. This project (*see* Figs 11.1 and 11.2) is based on a hanging worked and signed by 'Anne Grant 1750'. The original is at Monymusk in Aberdeenshire.

Conservatory Wall Hanging

Materials

Evenweave linen (35 count): 150 x 180mm (6 x 7in)

Stranded cotton as listed in colour key

Tapestry needle: No. 24 or 26

Small rectangular or round embroidery frame

Size

100 x 127mm (4 x 5in)

Fig 11.2 **Conservatory design.**

Conservatory Wall Hanging

		Skeins	DMC	Anchor	Madeira
	Coffee	1	3045	888	2103
	Dark cream	1	676	891	2208
	Light cream	1	677	886	2207
	Light green	1	320	216	1311
	Dark green	1	319	683	1313
	Grey	1	453	231	1806
	Dark pink	1	335	38	0610
	Light pink	1	3326	36	0606
	Dark blue	1	797	147	0912
	Light blue	1	799	145	0910
	Dark red	1	815	43	0512
	Red	1	321	47	0510
	Dark peach	1	352	9	0303
	Light peach	1	353	868	0304
	Bright yellow	1	307	289	0104
	Dark fawn	1	935	861	1507
	Mid fawn	1	437	362	2012
	Light fawn	1	739	1009	2014
	Ecru	1	Ecru	926	Ecru
	Black	1	310	Black	Black
	White	1	Blanc	White	White

Preparation

Mark the outside edges and vertical and horizontal centres with small tacking stitches. Mount in a rectangular frame as described in Chapter 13 (*see* page 161).

Working method

Refer to the chart in Fig 11.3 and stitch using one strand of stranded cotton and tent stitch throughout. Begin to stitch at the top centre edge and complete the 'bricks' and arches first.

Follow this by working the columns and the bottom two rows of floor tiles. When these are complete it is easier to count the threads to find the position for the rest of the details.

When the embroidery is finished, make up the hanging in one of the alternative ways given later in this chapter.

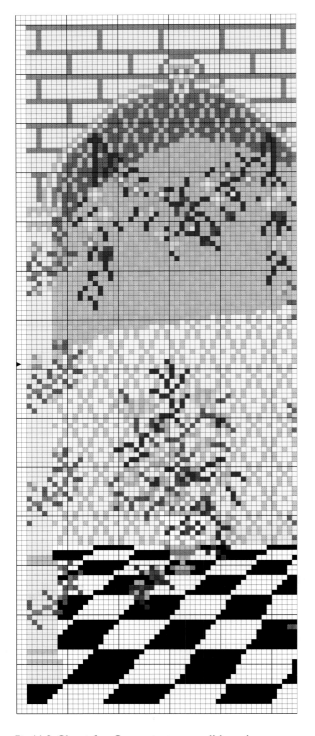

Fig 11.3 **Chart for Conservatory wall hanging.**

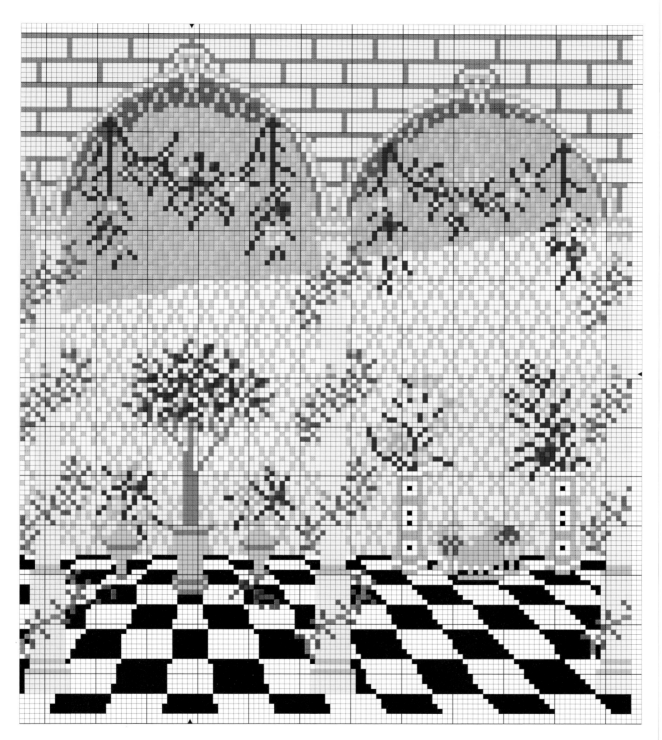

Fig 11.4 **Landscape wall hanging based on the design for a three-fold screen.**

Landscape Wall Hanging

A canvaswork wall hanging can be made using the chart for the Pastoral Landscape three-fold screen from Chapter 6 (*see* page 78), omitting the space between each panel.

Working method

Prepare the canvas and work the design as instructed for the Conservatory wall hanging. Begin to stitch at one of the lower corners. Make up the hanging following one of the methods given on page 157.

Landscape Wall Hanging

Materials

Evenweave linen (35 count): 150 x 180mm (6 x 7in)

Stranded cotton as listed in colour key

Tapestry needle: No. 24 or 26

Small rectangular or round embroidery frame

Size

126 x 95mm (5 x 3¾in)

Fig 11.5 **Crewel Work wall hanging mounted within Georgian panelling.**

Crewel Work Wall Hanging

The design for this wall hanging, shown in detail in Fig 11.6, is based on an eighteenth-century crewel work fragment. The strong Chinese influence makes it very suitable to the late Georgian or Regency period.

Fig 11.6 **Crewel Work design.**

Crewel Work Wall Hanging

Materials

Lightweight plain or patterned silk: 200 x 150mm (8 x 6in) or required size plus 50mm (2in) turning allowance OR

Cotton fabric with a patterned weave: 200 x 150mm (8 x 6in) or required size plus 50mm (2in) turning allowance

Stranded cotton as listed in colour key

Embroidery or quilting needle: No. 10

Size

150 x 90mm (6 x 3½in) or as required

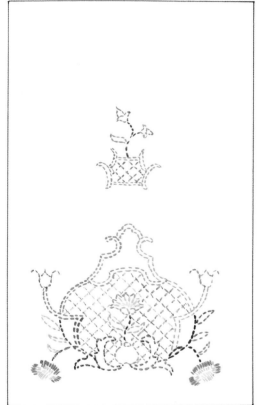

Fig 11.7 **Pattern for Crewel Work wall hanging.**

Fig 11.8 **Stitch pattern for Crewel Work wall hanging.**

Crewel Work Wall Hanging

		Skeins	DMC	Anchor	Madeira
	Dark peach	1	352	9	0303
	Light peach	1	353	868	0304
	Yellow	1	743	305	0113
	Dark green	1	3051	268	1508
	Light green	1	3053	260	1603
	Blue	1	799	145	0910

The design can be centred onto fabric and worked in a variety of sizes, or can be used as a repeat motif. It is also a suitable design for use on a bed cover, bed hangings or curtains.

Preparation

Mark the outer edge of your desired size for the design with small tacking stitches. Using the pattern from Fig 11.7, transfer the design to the fabric using either the tracing, dressmaker's carbon or photocopy method (*see* Chapter 14 – remember that the photocopy method will reverse the image). Mount the fabric in a small embroidery frame (*see* Chapter 13).

Working method

Work the design using the colour and stitch guide in Fig 11.8. Backstitch and small straight stitches should be used as indicated.

When the embroidery is complete, make up the hanging using one of the two alternative methods described below.

Making up wall hangings

Your embroidered wall hanging can be hung from a pole or incorporated within the panelling in a room.

Hanging from a pole

1 Trim the excess fabric from the sides and lower edge to about 10mm (⅜in) and from the top edge to about 20mm (¾in).

2 Turn the lower edge to the reverse side and secure with fabric glue or small stitches into the back of the embroidery.

3 Turn the two side edges under and secure it in the same way.

4 Fold the top edge of the fabric over to the reverse side and turn under 5mm (³⁄₁₆in) to make a hem. Secure with small stitches. This hem is used to hold the pole from which the hanging will be suspended.

Mounting within panelling

1 Make the moulding 'frame' to surround the hanging in the same way as shown for a picture frame in A of Fig 8.24 (*see* page 107). Use any miniature moulding without a rebate. Stain, paint or varnish as desired.

2 Follow the instructions for using a flat-backed moulding in Chapter 8 and Fig 8.25 (*see* page 108). The method used for mounting the hanging is the same – the hanging is just larger.

3 When the fabric has been mounted and the frame has been glued into position, allow the glue to dry completely.

4 With a sharp craft knife, cut the excess card and fabric from around the outer edges. You may need to colour the edges of the card to match the moulding. Apply any paint or stain very sparingly to avoid it bleeding into the edge of the fabric.

5 Finally, glue the framed panel into position on the wall of your house.

12 Working to 1/24 scale

Most of the projects in this book could be adapted to 1/24 scale. The working methods and general instructions remain the same.

Given that most of the items can, in full scale, vary in size considerably, it is not necessary that a 1/24-scale version should be exactly half the size of the 1/12-scale item. For example, samplers can be very small or quite large. A small 1/12 version worked on finer fabric could represent a large sampler in 1/24 scale.

Scaling work

Generally, projects can be worked on the same lightweight silk and cotton fabrics as recommended for 1/12 scale. Patterns and designs can be reduced to half size on a photocopier. Use one strand of stranded cotton or machine embroidery threads.

The machine-made rugs can be made to half size simply by working them to the desired 1/24 scale.

Curtain and blind patterns can be reduced as suggested above, as can the crewel work curtain design.

The crewel work patterns and designs for the cushions, wall hanging, screen and workbag are easily reduced to half size.

The crewel work bed hangings and bedcover and the gold bedcover can all be worked to half size by reducing the patterns as above.

The simulated patchwork bedcovers could also be reduced and painted successfully. The pieced patchwork would work as well.

The quilted designs could be reduced and simplified by leaving out some of the trellis lines and reducing the layers of muslin to two.

Counted thread work

Projects based on canvas or evenweave linen can be reduced in size by using a different count fabric, as suggested below.

Use one strand of stranded cotton or substitute machine embroidery threads.

Item	1/12 scale	1/24 scale
Carpets and rugs	24, 22, 18 canvas	35, 40 evenweave
Cushions	22 canvas	40 evenweave
	35 evenweave	80–120 silk gauze
Chair covers	35 evenweave	80–120 silk gauze
Footstools	35, 40 evenweave	80–120 silk gauze
Pictures	40 evenweave	80–120 silk gauze
Wall hangings	35 evenweave	80–120 silk gauze
Samplers	32, 35, 40 evenweave	80–120 silk gauze
Screens	35, 40 evenweave	80–120 silk gauze
Table top	40 evenweave	80–120 silk gauze
Bell pulls	35 evenweave	80–120 silk gauze
Rose and ribbon bed	27, 35 evenweave	40 evenweave
		80–120 silk gauze

13 Materials and working methods

Fabrics

Canvas

Canvas is available in various counts – the number of threads to 25mm (1in). The higher the number of threads, the finer the canvas.

Single-thread canvas, also known as mono canvas, is used for the projects in this book. This can be purchased in white, pale yellow or 'antique' brown.

Interlock canvas is white, with a twisted weave in one direction. It is more pliable than the normal weave. Interlock canvas can be cut to a shape without fraying.

Coin net is a cotton canvas with a 24 count.

Evenweaves

Evenweaves can be woven from linen, cotton or, less commonly, rayon. They are also sold in various counts.

Linen is the easiest fabric to work on as the linen threads are finer, which means the holes are larger by comparison.

Cotton evenweaves appear to be more closely woven because the cotton threads are thicker than linen and slightly fluffy, making the hole seem smaller.

Hardanger and Aida fabrics have threads which are woven in

blocks, forming 'squares'. Generally, these fabrics are too coarse for miniature work.

Silk

Habutai silk is a white silk fabric with a flat surface. It can be obtained in various weights, the lightest being ideal for miniature work.

Cotton

Lawn is a lightweight, smooth fabric which can be bought either plain or patterned. It is ideal for miniature projects.

Voile is lighter in weight than lawn and has a more open weave. Muslin is even more loosely woven than lawn or voile.

Wadding

Waddings come in various weights and thicknesses. Some are very fluffy and these are often too thick for miniature work. Others are more like a soft interlining and are more suitable for working to a miniature scale.

Domette is a light, knitted interlining with a brushed surface.

Felt, being a soft, compacted fabric, can be used effectively as a padding.

Embroidery frames

Most of the projects in this book will benefit from being worked in an embroidery frame. When working on canvas and evenweave fabrics, the frame will help to reduce distortion. It is also easier to be precise with the stitching when the fabric is stabilized in a frame.

There are various types of frame: slate frames, stretchers, card mounts and tambour (round) frames. Each requires a different method of preparation.

Slate frames

Slate frames are rectangular-shaped and consist of two sides with circular notches, into which the two rounded sides with webbing are fixed. Wing nuts at each corner tension the material, which can be adjusted by rolling the rounded sides. Fig 13.1 shows how to mount the fabric.

Fig 13.1 **Using a slate frame.**

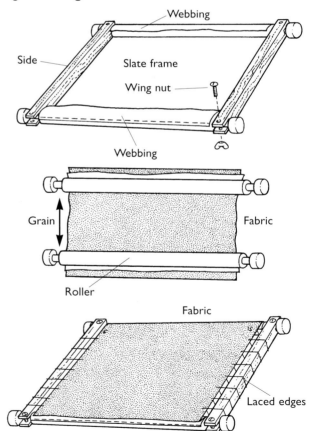

Dismantle the frame and lay the two webbing strips face down on two opposite sides of the fabric. Make sure the fabric is on the straight grain.

Stitch through the fabric and webbing using backstitch with a strong thread. Fasten on and off securely.

Locate the rounded sides in the notches in the square sides, and roll until the fabric is tensioned. Tighten the wing nuts.

Lace the fabric to the remaining two square sides with a strong thread to tension the fabric in both directions.

Stretchers

A simpler form of frame can be made by using artist stretchers, which are available in many sizes. The sides are purchased in pairs of the desired length, with tongue-and-groove ends which are simply pushed together.

It is also possible to buy a smaller version of these, usually as an assorted pack, made especially for embroiderers. These are very useful for working small projects (*see* Fig 13.2).

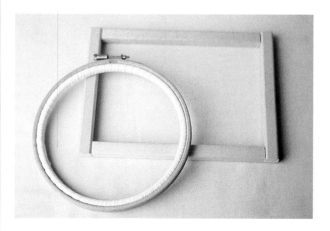

Fig 13.2 **A small stretcher and a round frame.**

Fig 13.3 **Using a stretcher.**

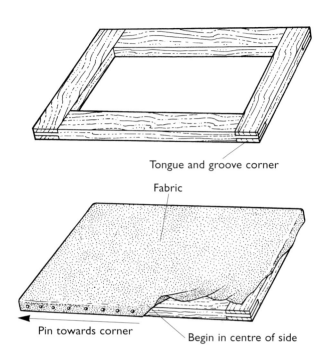

Tongue and groove corner

Fabric

Pin towards corner

Begin in centre of side

Alternatively, a home-made version can be made using angle brackets to hold the corners. Assemble the stretcher by pushing the corners together, making sure the frame is square at the corners. Fig 13.3 shows how to mount the fabric.

Using drawing pins or thumbtacks, pin the fabric along one of the longer sides, stretching the fabric slightly.

Then pin the opposite side, stretching the fabric slightly and making sure the grain of the fabric is straight across the centre.

Pin the remaining two sides in the same way, making sure that the grain of the fabric is straight at all times.

Card mounts

It is possible to cut a mount from sturdy card for very small pieces of fabric.

Choose a piece of card at least 10cm (4in) larger, in both directions than the piece of embroidery to be worked.

Mark and cut a window in the centre, leaving a border of 40mm (1½in) around the edges (*see* Fig 13.4).

On the reverse side of the card, spread a line of PVA glue around the centre opening. Allow to dry completely (*see* Fig 13.5).

Place the fabric over the opening, with the right side showing through to the right side of the card, and press around the opening with a warm iron. This will dry mount the fabric into the opening, ready for embroidery.

Fig 13.4 **Making a card frame for small pieces of fabric.**

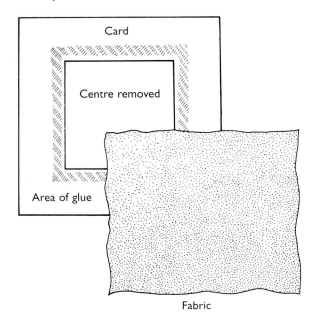

Fig 13.5 **Card mounts showing the reverse and the mount in use.**

Note: When mounting canvas in this way, it is necessary to place the canvas in position while the PVA glue is still wet, as canvas does not dry mount well. It is also advisable to be rather more generous with the glue when mounting canvas as opposed to other fabrics.

Tambour or round frames

These frames are made in wood or plastic. The wooden ones are best as the fabric does not slip, especially if the inner ring is covered with binding or strips of fabric (*see* Figs 13.6 and 13.2).

To mount the embroidery fabric, lay the inner ring down on a surface. Position the fabric over the inner ring. Push the outer ring onto the inner ring, pulling the fabric taut, and tighten the tensioning screw.

Fig 13.6 **A tambour or round frame.**

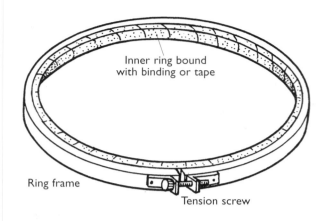

Inner ring bound
with binding or tape

Ring frame

Tension screw

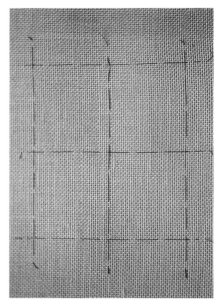

Fig 13.7 **Marking outlines and centres
with tacking thread.**

Spring frames

If you choose to embroider by machine, a
spring frame can be used which fits under the
foot of the machine more easily. This is a metal
sprung ring which fits into a plastic outer ring.

When fitting fabric for machine embroidery,
lay the outer ring on a surface. Position the
fabric over the outer ring. Push the inner ring
into the outer ring, pulling the fabric taut. The
inner spring frame will hold the fabric taut
while you stitch.

Beginning to stitch

Most of the projects require the fabric to be
marked with small tacking stitches to show
the outer edges and the vertical and
horizontal centres.

On canvas and evenweave fabrics this can be
done easily by following the weave of the fabric
(*see* Fig 13.7). On other fabrics this can be
achieved by cutting out a paper pattern as a

guide, or by using the trace and tack method
described in Chapter 14 (*see* page 166).

Using a chart

On most of the charts each square is solid
colour. This indicates one individual stitch,
usually tent or cross stitch as stated in the
working instructions.

Some of the sampler charts show the use of
both solid squares and lines within or on the
edge of a square. Each line indicates the
position of a small straight stitch, over one
thread, in the direction of the line on the chart.

Working on canvas and evenweave

To begin, make a knot in the end of the
embroidery thread and take the thread through

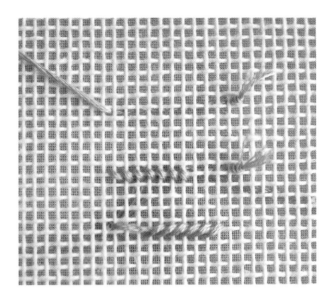

Fig 13.8 **Beginning with a knot
(front and reverse shown).**

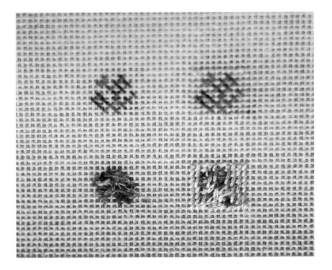

Fig 13.9 **Stitching on canvas
(front and reverse shown).**

the canvas or evenweave, from the front, about 15mm (½in) from where the first stitch is to be made. Bring the thread back through the canvas or evenweave at the position of the first stitch.

Proceed with the stitching, which will eventually cover the length of thread on the back between the knot and the first stitch. The knot on the front of the work can then be cut away (*see* Fig 13.8).

Many charts require stitches to be spaced about. Using the colour required, work the stitches as indicated on the chart, taking the thread across the back of the canvas as necessary. When an area of design has been worked, the background can be filled in, covering all the threads on the back (*see* Fig 13.9).

14 Methods of transferring designs

Dressmakers' carbon

This is a form of carbon paper used by dressmakers to outline patterns. The carbon comes in blue, red, white and yellow and washes out after use.

The carbon is placed face down onto the fabric with the design placed on top. The lines of the design can then be traced onto the fabric. I find that a worn-out biro gives a good line as it is harder than a pencil.

Care should be taken not to smudge the carbon by pressing on it with your fingers.

Trace and tack

This is a good method for larger, simple designs, especially for putting the basic outline of a shape onto the fabric.

Trace the outline onto tissue paper. Then lay the tissue paper onto the fabric and stitch through the lines with a large running stitch and tacking cotton. Fasten on and off securely. Carefully tear off the tissue paper, leaving the stitches to mark the shape.

Tracing through fabric

Some fabrics are fine enough to see through when laid on top of a design. This is usually possible if the design has been drawn in black ink or is on a printed page.

Lay the fabric over the design and, with a fabric transfer pencil or soluble pen (*see* below), trace the lines of the design onto the fabric.

Embroidery transfer pencils

The purpose of a transfer pencil is literally to create a transfer, i.e., to trace a design onto paper which can then be ironed off onto fabric. The pencil line will wash out after use.

These pencils can also be used directly onto the fabric. Always have a very sharp point as this gives a fine line which will be hidden by the stitchery and may not need to be washed out on completion of the work.

Remember that if the iron-off method is used, the design will be reversed.

Soluble pens

Water-soluble and air-soluble pens are widely used by embroiderers. They are similar to a felt-tip pen, usually giving a pink or blue line.

The water-soluble ink can be removed with a damp cotton bud after use, or by washing the completed item if that is feasible. The air-soluble pens should only be used for very short-term pieces, as the ink disappears within a few hours.

Transfer with photocopies

A design can be photocopied onto paper and the resulting copy can then be ironed off onto fabric. This method works better on fabrics of natural fibres, i.e. cotton or silk. Some synthetics are resistant, but it is always worth trying.

This method reverses the design, but it has the advantage of being very quick and simple.

A colour photocopy can be made directly onto fabric or canvas. This can be used to produce 'tapestries' or wall hangings, etc. Fine calico is a good base to use.

For designs embroidered in counted thread, evenweave or canvas is required. Use the colour copy as a guide, placing the correctly coloured stitches directly over it.

The designs can usually be enlarged or reduced with considerable precision, so it is possible to recreate the exact scale.

Once the photocopy is on the fabric, the embroidery can be worked as if on a printed canvas, in tent or cross stitch.

15 Bonding methods and colouring techniques

Bonding methods

Bond-a-web

Bond-a-web is a brand name for a web of adhesive which is supported by non-stick paper. It can be used to bond two fabrics together, or to bond fabric to paper or card.

The Bond-a-web is placed onto the reverse side of the fabric with the adhesive next to the fabric, i.e., paper side uppermost. An iron is used to bond the adhesive, set to the correct heat for the fabric.

Once the Bond-a-web and the fabric have bonded, the paper can be removed from the back of the Bond-a-web. The fabric can then be turned over and bonded in the same way to another surface.

It is a good idea to have a piece of non-stick baking paper on the ironing surface, and between the iron and the piece being bonded, to protect the work surface and iron.

Bonding powder

This is a powdered form of Bond-a-web adhesive which is used by embroiderers when small or scattered areas are to be bonded for creative effects.

The powder is sprinkled over the surface and small fragments of thread or fabric are then added. A sheet of non-stick paper is placed over the whole surface and pressed with an iron.

Bonded interlinings

There are several brands of bonded interlining available. Some are woven and some, like Vilene, are a fused fabric.

The interlining has a web of adhesive on one side which can be used to stiffen fabric or to prevent fabric fraying.

The interlinings come in various weights, the lightest being ultra-light and the heaviest pelmet weight. An iron is used to bond the lining to the fabric; it should be set to the correct heat for the fabric being used.

Adhesives

The only safe adhesive to use with fabric is one with a PVA base. This is basically a plastic glue which, when dry, will not change with time. Other glues with rubber or solvent bases are best avoided.

PVA adhesives come in various strengths. Wood glue is very strong; fabric glue is more dilute. These glues can be diluted further with water. Wood glue is hard when dry, fabric glue remains pliable.

The wood glue can be used for dry mounting. A thin layer of glue is applied to a card, wood or paper surface and left to dry completely. The fabric can then be bonded with an iron to the dry area of glue. If the placement is not initially correct, apply the iron again and peel off the fabric.

Fabric dyes and paints

There are many different types of fabric paint and dye available. Some are for particular fabrics, e.g. silk dyes for silk, special dyes for natural fibres, others for synthetics. If the correct type is used and the individual manufacturer's instructions are followed for use and fixing, the resulting fabric should be washable. If the item is never going to be washed, as with most miniature pieces, any dyes or paints can be used on any fabric, even artists' watercolours.

Some fabrics, for example linen, which have a high level of natural oils or dressing may require more than one application of colour.

When colouring a small area, the dye or paint is best applied with a brush rather than immersing the fabric. Place the fabric in a frame so that it is taut and smooth. Apply the dye or paint with a small brush. Leave to dry in the frame on a level surface so that the dye dries evenly. A completed piece of work can be 'antiqued' by painting on a solution of cold black tea. Test on a spare piece of fabric first to see how it turns out.

Painting freehand

If you are unable to find a suitable fabric, or wish to reproduce some of the projects as a painted surface, this can be achieved by painting directly onto fabric.

Fabric paints are available which are thicker in consistency than those which are water based. These paints can be applied to fabric without the paint bleeding because the paint stays on the surface of the fabric. For fine details use a size 0 or 00 pointed paintbrush. When the completed piece is ironed, the colours will be fast and washable.

Watercolour and acrylic paints can also be used. As these are water based, the amount of paint loaded onto the brush must be carefully considered. The brush needs to be wet enough to take up the paint, but not so wet that the fabric absorbs any water. This is sometimes called 'dry brush technique'. It works best on a fine, smooth fabric such as cotton or silk and, although colourfast to light will not be washable (*see* Fig 15.1).

Fig 15.1 **A design painted onto fabric with watercolour paints. Fabric paints will produce the same effect.**

Fabric transfer paints

There are several brands of fabric transfer paint available, but all will have the word 'transfer' somewhere on the label. They are made for use on synthetic fabrics, on which they give the brightest colours. When used on natural fibres the colours are softer.

Transfer paints and dyes are painted onto paper and then ironed off onto fabric. Remember that this will reverse the design (*see* Fig 15.2).

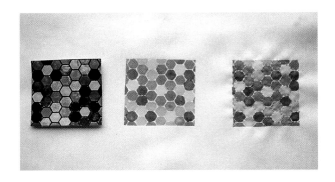

Fig 15.2 **The use of transfer paints and dyes.**

There is sometimes a considerable difference in the colours when they have been ironed off onto the fabric. A sample strip should be made first to see the colour before using on the actual piece.

A photocopy of the design can be used. Colour this with the transfer paints and iron off, with the iron set at the correct heat for the fabric.

Alternatively, a tracing onto detail paper can be used. Tracing paper itself is not successful. Detail paper, sometimes marketed as 'marker pads', is a white, opaque paper that is see-through when placed over a design.

When ironing off the transfer, move the iron gently and smoothly so that the paper remains in the same place. It may take several minutes for the colour to transfer onto some fabrics. Place a piece of paper under the fabric to protect the working surface.

16 Finishing methods

Making tassels

The tassel should initially be made longer than required as it is easier to handle.

Working method

1 Cut a piece of stiff card into a rectangle 100 x 60mm (4 x 2⅜in), then cut a piece from the centre 50 x 30mm (2 x 1³⁄₁₆in). Mark the centre line and cut a small notch in one end of the card to secure the threads (*see* Fig 16.1A).

2 Wind the thread around the card until the required thickness of tassel is achieved. Do not make the tassel too thick, as it will look out of scale (*see* Fig 16.1B).

3 Bind the middle 10–15mm (⅜–½in) of the tassel using the centre mark as a guide. Cut the threads at each end of the card (*see* Fig 16.1C).

4 Bend the tassel in half and bind the head to form a loop. Finally, trim the ends of the threads to the required length: probably 10–15mm (⅜–½in) (*see* Fig 16.1D).

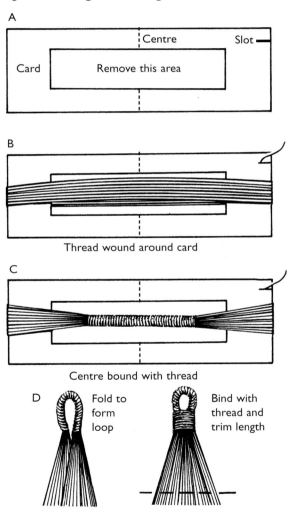

Fig 16.1 **The stages in making a tassel.**

A

Card Centre Slot

Remove this area

B

Thread wound around card

C

Centre bound with thread

D Fold to form loop   Bind with thread and trim length

171

Making fringes

Here are two methods of making miniature fringes. The first is based on a strip of fabric, the second is a knotted edging.

Working method: fabric fringes

Almost any fine fabric can be used, eg, silk, cotton and linen.

1 Cut a strip of fabric about 50mm (2in) wide and at least 100mm (4in) longer than the required length of fringed edging.

2 Work two rows of straight machine stitching, close together, down the length of the strip of fabric and along the straight grain. The example in Fig 16.2. has been stitched in a contrasting thread for clarity.

3 Trim away the excess fabric along the upper edge, close to the stitching.

4 Set the machine to a zigzag stitch and a short stitch length. Machine along the strip over the straight stitching, enclosing the top edge. A perle cotton or fine braid can be incorporated at this stage if desired.

5 Trim the lower edge of the fabric to the required width of the fringe.

6 Fray the fabric back to the machine stitching, removing one thread at a time.

7 Stitch or glue the fringe into position on the item to be decorated.

Working method: knotted fringes

1 Turn under the edge of the fabric or canvas.

2 Cut the thread or cord into lengths. A manageable length is about 100mm (4in).

3 Fold these lengths in half and pull them through the edge of the hem with a fine crochet hook to form a loop (*see* Fig 16.3).

4 Slip the two ends of the thread down through the loop and pull them firmly to tighten the knot.

5 Trim the threads to the desired length when the whole row of knots has been completed.

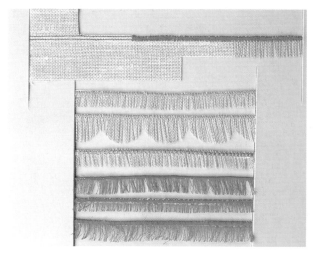

Fig 16.2 **Making a fabric fringe.**

Fig 16.3 **Making a knotted fringe.**

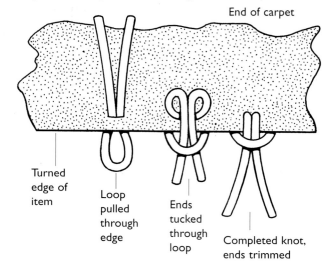

End of carpet

Turned edge of item

Loop pulled through edge

Ends tucked through loop

Completed knot, ends trimmed

Blocking embroidery

Counted-thread embroidery on linen or canvas often distorts with the tension of the stitches. The use of a frame will help to prevent this, but you may need to block the finished embroidery back into shape.

Before blocking, make sure all threads used are colourfast, and test any painted backgrounds to make sure the dyes are fixed. Moisten a small corner and blot with tissue to see if any colour transfers to the tissue.

Blocking

Materials

Pinboard or similar, soft enough to take drawing pins
  or thumbtacks
Paper
Transparent plastic sheeting
Drawing pins or thumbtacks
Waterproof pen

Working method

1 Draw a rectangle on a sheet of paper using the waterproof pen. Make sure all the corners are true right angels. This rectangle should be larger than the embroidery, as it is there to provide straight lines to follow when pinning out the fabric.

2 Lay the paper on the pinboard and cover it with the sheet of plastic.

3 Trim any excess fabric from the edges of the embroidery, leaving enough turnings, 20mm (¾in) minimum, to allow for the drawing pins.

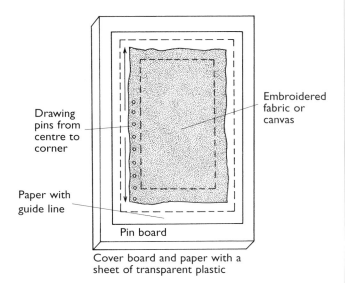

Drawing pins from centre to corner

Embroidered fabric or canvas

Paper with guide line

Pin board

Cover board and paper with a sheet of transparent plastic

Fig 16.4 **Blocking a completed piece of canvaswork into shape.**

4 With a small damp cloth or sponge, dampen the embroidery and the surrounding canvas or linen.

5 Lay the embroidery within the paper rectangle and begin pinning the fabric to the board, from the middle of one side to the corner, stretching the fabric slightly as you work. Use the line on the paper as a guide (*see* Fig 16.4).

6 Return to the middle of the side and work towards the other corner in the same way.

7 Repeat the process along the opposite side, pulling the fabric so that the grain is straight.

8 Repeat again on the two remaining sides.

9 Leave the piece to dry naturally, lying flat in an even temperature.

10 When completely dry, remove the pins. Occasionally, if the piece was very badly distorted, the process may need to be repeated.

Mitred corners

Working a mitred corner will help to cut down unnecessary bulk.

Working method

1 Trim the seam allowance.

2 Cut a small amount from the corner of the fabric (*see* Fig 16.5A).

3 Fold the corner down diagonally.

4 Fold the adjacent sides once, and then again to form a hem (*see* Fig 16.5B and C). Secure with tiny hemming stitches.

Fig 16.5 **Making a mitred corner.**

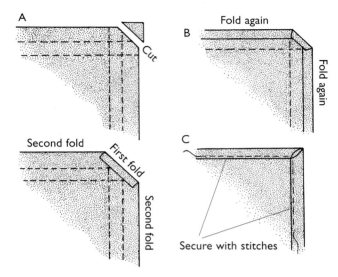

Fastening on

The old rule that 'thou shalt not start with a knot' derives from a time when most embroidered articles had to be laundered, and a knot would unravel in the washing process.

With miniatures, which are unlikely to need repeated washing, it is sometimes an advantage to begin with a small knot. However, the best method, once some stitching has been worked, is to secure the beginning of the thread into the back of the existing stitching.

On an evenweave fabric or canvas use the advance knot method, described in Chapter 13 (*see* page 164), until an area of stitching has been worked, after which the above method can be used.

A third method is described below under Darning on Net.

Backstitch

Backstitch is used for working a smooth line.

Bring the needle through from the back of the fabric and take it down again to give the length of stitch required. Bring the needle up through the fabric again, the length of a stitch away from the previous stitch (at A), then take the needle back through the fabric, next to the previous stitch (B).

When complete, fasten off into the back of the stitches.

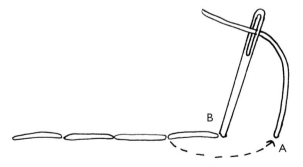

Blanket or buttonhole stitch

These stitches can be used to form an edging or a row of stitching, and can be radiated to form a flower effect.

For blanket stitch, bring the needle through from the back of the fabric at A, and take it down at B, a little to one side of A, to give the desired length and direction of stitch. Bring the needle back through at C, in line with B, making sure the thread is behind the needle. Continue in this way, bringing the needle up at D, to the right or left of C, and down at E, in line with D, keeping the thread behind the needle.

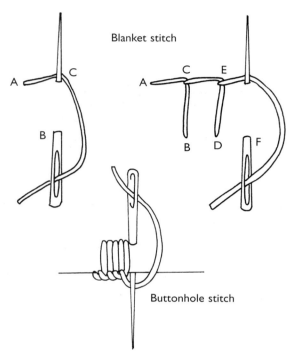

Blanket stitch

Buttonhole stitch

When complete, fasten off into the back of the stitches.

Buttonhole stitch is worked in the same way, but with the stitches very close together.

Couching

In couching, a thread is laid on the surface of the fabric and then stitched down with a second, finer thread.

Bring the thread to be laid through from the back of the fabric. Threaded in a second needle, bring the sewing thread through from the back, immediately beside the first thread (A), and take a stitch over the first thread and down

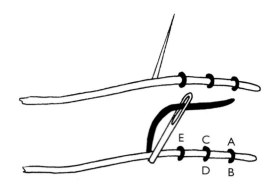

close to the other side (B). Continue to secure the first thread in this manner, at the same time moving the first thread, if necessary, to form the shape or line required.

Fasten the sewing thread off behind the stitching, then take the first thread through to the back and fasten it off.

Cross stitch

The diagram shows the method for working a row of cross stitch by making the first half of each stitch all the way along the row and then working the second half on the way back along the row.

For the first row, bring the needle up at A, down at B, up at C, down at D and so on until the row is as long as you require. Then, work back along the row crossing over these first stitches, by bringing the needle up at M, down at N, up at O, down at P and so on, until all the stitches have been crossed.

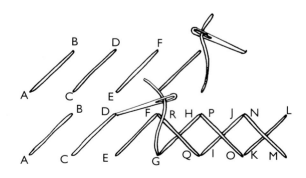

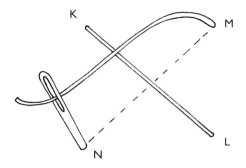

A second method is to work each cross stitch in full as you go. For one stitch, following the diagram, bring the needle up at K, down at L, up at M and down at N. Which method you choose will depend on the design.

Fasten off in the back of the stitching.

Cushion stitch

Cushion stitch forms a square of diagonal stitches. Each alternate square has the stitches sloping in the opposite direction. The squares are over three threads in the project included in this volume (*see* page 14).

The first stitch is worked diagonally over one thread (up at A and down at B), the second over two (up at C and down at D), and the third over three (up at E, down at F). The fourth stitch is worked over two threads (up at G, down at H) and the final stitch over one (up at I, down at J), thus forming a square.

First stitch   Second stitch   Third stitch   Fourth stitch

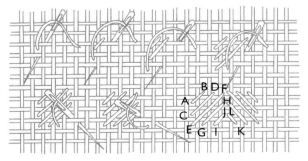

To begin working the next square, bring the needle up at K as shown, and take it down at L.

Darning

For this stitch a tapestry needle must be used. In this book it is used only on evenweave fabrics or canvas to facilitate counting. It produces a regular pattern.

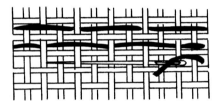

Bring the needle through from the back of the fabric and take it down again, having passed over the required number of threads. Pass under the required number of threads before bringing the needle up again, and continue in this way to the end of the row. In the diagram, the thread is passed over three and under one.

Usually, rows of stitches are worked in every row of holes in the fabric/canvas, though empty rows can be left in between.

Fasten off into the back of the stitching.

Darning on net

Darning stitch on net is worked by weaving the thread through the holes in the net fabric to form the required pattern.

Photocopy, trace or draw the design on paper, and tack the piece of net into position over the design.

Begin by taking the needle through the holes of the net, leaving an end of about 25mm (1in).

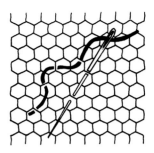

Proceed to darn in and out of the holes, following the design. For miniature work, always darn in and out of adjacent holes.

When an area is complete, simply cut the thread off close to the net and leave, trimming the starting end in the same way. When the whole design is complete, remove the netting from the paper pattern and cut the item to shape.

Detached chain stitch

This stitch is useful for working flowers and leaves. Working a short stitch produces a rounded shape while a longer stitch produces a narrower oval shape.

Bring the needle through from the back of the fabric (A), then take it down as close as possible to the same point (B). Bring the needle up again at C, making a stitch of the length required, and looping the thread under the needle. Pull the thread through and take a small stitch over the loop to secure it (D).

Fasten off into the back of the stitching.

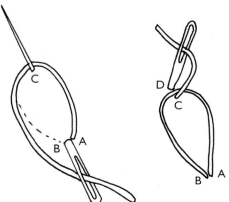

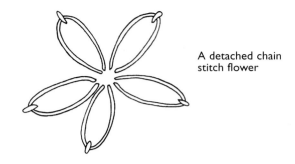

A detached chain stitch flower

Feather stitch

Feather stitching can be used to give a decorative outline. Bring the needle through from the back of the fabric to come up at A, and take it down at B. Before pulling the thread through, bring the needle up again at C and loop the thread under the needle. Draw the thread through. Take the needle down at D and up at E in the same way, again looping the thread under the needle. Continue in this way until the required number of stitches have been worked.

When complete, take a small stitch over the last loop to secure.

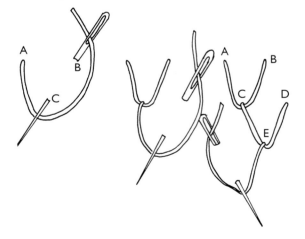

French knot

This stitch can be used alone or in clusters. They add texture to a piece. Bring the needle through from the back of the fabric and wind the thread once around the needle. Take the point of the needle back through the fabric, very close to where the thread was brought through to the front. Draw the thread through to form a neat, compact knot.

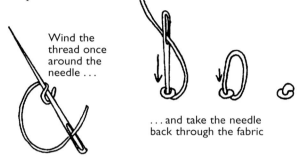

Wind the thread once around the needle ...

...and take the needle back through the fabric

Hemming

Hemming stitch is used to secure hems. Turn the edge of the fabric over as desired. Pick up a little of the fabric and the turned hem with the needle and draw the thread through, repeating until all of the hem has been secured. Only a tiny stitch should show on the right side, so it is an advantage to use a very fine needle.

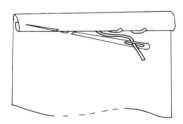

Herringbone stitch

Herringbone stitch is generally used to give a decorative border, but can also be used as a filling stitch.

Bring the needle through from the back of the fabric to come up at A, then take it down at B to form a diagonal stitch. Bring the needle

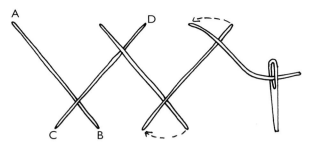

back up at C, to one side of B, then make another diagonal stitch to cross over the first. Continue in this way until the desired number of stitches have been worked.

Fasten off into the back of the stitching.

Running stitch

This stitch is basically the same as darning, but it is worked on a plain fabric rather than a counted fabric, and has the spaces and stitches of equal length. It can be used for outlining and in quilting.

Take the needle in and out of the fabric to form stitches and spaces, all of a uniform length, in the line or shape required.

Length of space is equivalent to length of stitch

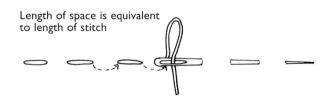

If the stitch is used for quilting, a smaller stitch can be obtained by stab stitching. Take the needle through the fabrics and draw the thread through, then, in a second movement, bring the needle and thread back through the fabrics again. Work each stitch in two movements.

Satin stitch

This stitch is used as a filling for small areas. Bring the needle through from the back of the fabric, at any point on the outline. Take the needle back through the fabric on the opposite side of the shape, and then up again very close to the first stitch. Continue to place stitches next to one another in this manner until the shape is filled. Fasten off into the back of the stitching.

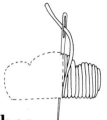

Seeding stitches

Seeding is an effect created by short, straight stitches scattered at various angles. Traditionally, two stitches are used side by side, but for miniature work a single stitch is sufficient.

Simply work short stitches of equal length at angles to each other, clustered together.

Straight stitch

Straight stitch is the most basic and versatile embroidery stitch. It can be used for tiny leaves or flowers. It is simply a single stitch which can be of any length, and used side by side or set at an angle to radiate.

Bring the needle through from the back of the fabric and take it down again to make a stitch of the length required. Continue laying stitches in this way to give the effect that you require.

Tent stitch

By using tent stitch rather than half cross stitch, the stitches can be worked in any direction and look exactly the same on the front. Tent stitch also prevents the thread from slipping behind the weave of the fabric and disappearing, as it tends to with half cross stitch.

The diagram shows the sequence of stitches for working in different directions. Bring the needle through from the back of the fabric at the odd numbers and take it down through the even numbers. The top diagram shows the placing of the needle.

When rows are worked next to one another, the same holes are used as the previous row – do not leave a thread of canvas empty in between.

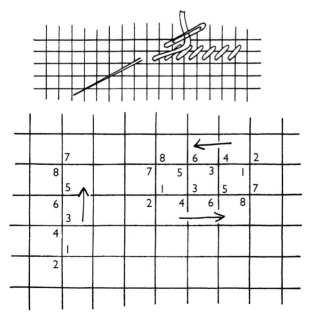

Sources of information

Museums

Most large towns and cities have a museum with a display of decorative arts that includes embroidered items. Many museums cover social history, showing the way people lived and the artifacts they used in their everyday lives. Some even have authentic room settings with furnishings of a particular period. Such things provide valuable general information.

If you want specific information, it is best to write to the curator in advance, stating exactly what you wish to know. A short list of clear questions will almost always bring a prompt response, but a general 'Tell me all you know about beds/chairs/Georgian houses/etc' rarely gets a reply.

In most countries, a list of museums and historical houses is published, usually updated every couple of years or so. Libraries have copies of these or lists of their own, and sometimes a section devoted to local history.

The brief list which follows is a starting point, indicating museums which have collections of Victorian historical embroidery and, in some cases, furnishings.

United Kingdom and Ireland

Geffrye Museum
Kingsland Road
London E2 8EA
0171 739 8368/9893

Room settings.

The Embroiderers' Guild
Apartment 41
Hampton Court Palace
East Molesey
Surrey KT8 9AU
0181 943 1229

Historical embroidery.
(By appointment only.)
The Guild have branches throughout the UK and Ireland, the USA, Canada and Australia.

Victoria and Albert Museum
Cromwell Road
London SW7
0171 938 8500

Embroidery, costume and furniture.

William Morris Gallery
The Water House
Lloyd Park
Forest Road
Walthamstow
London E17
0181 527 3782

Arts and Crafts textiles and furnishings.

Bowes Museum
Barnard Castle
Co. Durham DL12 8NP
01833 690606

Embroidery, costume and furnishings.

The American Museum
Claverton Manor
Bath
Avon BA2 7BD
01225 460503

Room settings.

Fitzwilliam Museum
Trumpington Street
Cambridge
Cambridgeshire CB2 1RB
01223 332900

Embroidery, mostly samplers.

Guildford Museum
Castle Arch
Guildford
Surrey GU1 3SX
01483 444750

Embroidery.

Maidstone Museum and Art Gallery
St Faith's Street
Maidstone
Kent ME14 1LH
01622 754497

Embroidery and furnishings.

Whitworth Art Gallery
University of Manchester
Oxford Road
Manchester
Greater Manchester M15 6ER
0161 275 7450

Fabrics and furnishings.

Costume Museum
51 Castlegate
Nottingham
Nottinghamshire NG1 6AF
0115 915 3500/5555

Costume, embroidery and lace.

York Castle Museum
The Eye of York
York
Yorkshire YO1 9RY
01904 653611

Room settings.

Royal Museum
Chambers Street
Edinburgh EH1 1JF
Scotland
0131 225 7534

Embroidery and furnishings.

The Burrell Collection
Pollok Country Park
2060 Pollokshaws Road
Glasgow G43 1AT
Scotland
0141 649 7151

Embroideries and tapestries.

Cardiff Castle
Castle Street
Cardiff CF1 2RB
South Glamorgan
01222 878 100

Arts and Crafts movement furniture and artifacts.

Ulster Folk and Transport Museum
153 Bangor Road
Cultra
Holywood
Co. Down BT18 0EU
Northern Ireland
01232 428428

Textiles and crafts.

Ulster Museum
Botanic Gardens
Stranmillis Road
Belfast BT9 5AB
Northern Ireland
01232 383000

Costume and lace.

National Museum of Ireland
Kildare Street and
7–9 Merrion Row
  and Merrion Street
Dublin 2
Republic of Ireland
003531 6777 444

Decorative arts and lace.

United States of America and Canada

The Baltimore Museum of Art
Art Museum Drive
Baltimore
Maryland 21218
410 396 6300

Quilts and household items.

Museum of Fine Arts
465 Huntington Avenue
Boston
Massachusetts 02115
617 267 9300

Large collection of textiles.

The Art Institute of Chicago
Michigan Avenue
    at Adams Street
Chicago
Illinois 60603
312 443 3600

Large collection of textiles.

The Farmers' Museum and Fenimore House
PO Box 800
Cooperstown
New York 13326
607 547 1450

Bedcovers and carpets.

Historic Deerfield Inc.
PO Box 321
Deerfield
Massachusetts 01342
413 774 5581

Household items.

Indianapolis Museum of Art
1200 West 38th Street
Indianapolis
Indiana 46208
317 923 1331

Eighteenth and nineteenth century embroidery.

The Brooklyn Museum
200 Eastern Parkway
Brooklyn
New York City
New York 11238
718 638 5000

Costume, bedhangings and window hangings.

The Metropolitan Museum of Art
1000 Fifth Avenue
5th Avenue at 82nd Street
New York City
New York 10028
212 879 5500

Costume and embroidery.

Philadelphia Museum of Art
Box 7646
Philadelphia
Pennsylvania 19101
215 763 8100

American and English embroideries.

National Museum of History and Technology
Smithsonian Institution
14th Street and Constitution Avenue
Washington DC 20560
202 357 2700

Coverlets and embroideries.

Royal Ontario Museum
100 Queens Park
Toronto
Ontario M5S 2C6
416 586 5549

Large collection of embroidery and lace.

Note: Many Canadian museums specialize in folk textiles, but may have small collections of Victorian embroidery.

Historic houses

These houses, which are well documented in books, magazines and libraries, are a good source of reference. Some are dedicated and restored to one particular era, but many have been added to over the centuries. Textiles, furnishings and sometimes embroideries are shown in context within room settings.

In most countries there are heritage organizations to care for these estates and houses, such as the National Trust and English Heritage in the United Kingdom. Please consult telephone directories and Tourist Information Offices for information on local organizations and houses.

Booklets or postcards from these organizations are usually available.

Books

Information and illustrations on embroidery, interior decoration, restoring period houses, furniture and decorative art styles can be found in books. There are also many specialist periodicals available which cover these areas. Your local reference library, or a browse in a large book shop, are good starting points.

The brief list which follows includes some books which may be out of print, but can be seen at libraries or purchased from secondhand book dealers.

Artley, Alexandra (Editor), *Putting Back the Style*, Ward Lock, London, UK, 1988
ISBN 07063 6708 1

Benn, Elizabeth (Editor), *Treasures from the Embroiderers' Guild Collection*, David & Charles, Devon, UK, 1991
ISBN 07153 9829 6

Johnson, Pauline, *Three Hundred Years of Embroidery, 1600–1900*, Wakefield Press in association with the Embroiderers' Guild of South Australia and The Embroiderers' Guild, Hampton Court Palace, Surrey, UK, 1987
ISBN 0949268 81X

Miller, Judith and Martin, *Period Details*, Mitchell Beazley, London, UK, 1988
ISBN 085533 6501

Parissien, Steven, *The Georgian Group Book of the Georgian House*, Aurum Press Ltd, London, UK, 1995
ISBN 085410 466 7

Swain, Margaret, *Scottish Embroidery, Medieval to Modern*, B. T. Batsford Ltd, London, UK, 1986
ISBN 07134 4638 2

Vince, John, *The Country House, How it Worked*, John Murray (Publishers) Ltd, London, UK, 1991
ISBN 07195 4769 5

Warner, Pamela, *Embroidery: A History*, B. T. Batsford Ltd, London, UK, 1991
ISBN 07134 61063

About the author

Pamela Warner's interest in embroidery began in the mid-1950s with her studies for a National Design Diploma (NDD) in fashion — which included embroidery — at Bromley College of Art.

After a career in banking and computing, followed by marriage and a family, Pamela rediscovered creative embroidery at an evening class. She went on to qualify and by 1979 was teaching embroidery for Bromley Adult Education and the Inner London Education Authority (ILEA). During the early 1980s she became involved as a tutor for City and Guilds embroidery classes at Bromley, and eventually took on full responsibility for the course. This continues to be her main occupation, along with working as an external verifier for the City and Guilds examination board. In 1999, Pamela formulated a syllabus for City and Guilds, enabling embroiderers to achieve a certificate in Miniature Embroidery.

Pamela discovered dolls' houses in 1989. She began with a ready-made house and a kit, but was soon frustrated with the small rooms. In order to learn the craft herself, she went on a Dolls' House Holiday, with Peter Alden, and was so impressed with the results that she keeps returning.

Pamela's work as a professional embroiderer has been exhibited widely, and she has undertaken many commissions for ecclesiastic and secular pieces. She has also spent 15 years restoring and conserving embroideries for Westminster Abbey and other churches.

This is Pamela's third book, following *Embroidery: A History* and *Miniature Embroidery for the Victorian Dolls' House*, as well as a series of booklets on the history of embroidery.

Index